Bristol Pub

GOD
AND THE
OVAL OFFICE

*The Religious Faith of Our
43 Presidents*

JOHN McCOLLISTER

W PUBLISHING GROUP™
www.wpublishinggroup.com

*A Division of Thomas Nelson, Inc.
www.ThomasNelson.com*

Published by W Publishing Group, a Division of Thomas Nelson, Inc., P.O. Box 141000, Nashville, Tennessee, 37214.

W Publishing Group books may be purchased in bulk for educational, busi-ness, fundraising, or sales promotional use. For information, please email SpecialMarkets@ThomasNelson.com.

All Scripture quotations are taken from The King James Version of the Bible (KJV).

Library of Congress Cataloging-in-Publication Data

McCollister, John.
    God and the Oval Office / by John McCollister.
        p. cm.
    Summary: "Presents information regarding each United States president and how their faith influenced them"—Provided by publisher.

    ISBN 0-8499-0405-6 (hardcover)

1. Presidents—United States—Religion.   I. Title.
BR516.M377 2005
973'.099—dc22   2005000301

Printed in the United States of America
05 06 07 08 09 RRD 9 8 7 6 5 4 3 2 1

CONTENTS

CONTENTS

PREFACE

It's a hot topic of conversation these days. Seldom is anyone neutral on the issue.

Politicians fill the air with impassioned rhetoric before cheering crowds. Pastors, priests, and rabbis pound pulpits to emphasize their points. Liberal watchdogs carry picket signs and protest in front of city hall.

Why are these advocates so zealous in their demonstrations? It's because they are involved in a controversy that has been debated for more than two centuries. In this experiment of democracy known as America, what is the proper blending of government and religion?

On one side of the question stand those who proclaim that faith in Almighty God and the heart of America are inseparable. "Our nation," they say, "was, and has been, honed on religious principles." They point to the fact that the framers of the Constitution and the Declaration of Independence not only referred to God, but also proclaimed the importance of divine support for the new nation. Some of those who support a melding of faith and government go so far as to say that America is first and foremost a Christian nation.

On the flip side are those who believe that we should forbid any connection whatsoever between church and state. They openly challenge, for example, the legality of displaying a plaque of the Ten Commandments on government property or religious symbols such as a cross or manger scene during the Christmas season in front of city hall. They even abhor any reference to God in the Pledge of Allegiance recited by students enrolled in public schools.

As with most other issues that evoke emotions, extremists on both sides have been overzealous in their attempts to convince others to agree with them. Couple this with the fact that so many attempt to reconstruct history in order to justify their personal prejudices, and the picture becomes more distorted.

If we consider only the facts, we must admit that the United States of America was not formed as a haven "for Christians only." True, the dominant religion in the nation has been Christianity. At the same time, the founders of the Republic were careful not to create a "religious state" or a "state religion." Instead they framed a nation that would allow, among other things, an opportunity for everyone to express his or her religious convictions without fear of government interference.

It should come as no surprise that the First Amendment to the Constitution guaranteed that no one particular religious denomination shall never prevail over the government. That same amendment also assured Americans that no governmental body will ever be able to control any free expression of faith.

To those who insist that we must heed the demand of the Constitution for the "separation of church and state," we call their attention to two things.

First, that specific phrase never appears in the Constitution. Instead, it is a comment borrowed from a personal letter written to a friend by our third president, Thomas Jefferson.

Second, and more importantly, the government of these United

States was built upon a spiritual foundation. Its major concepts are derived from the biblical teachings about the value and destiny of human beings. In other nations during the eighteenth century, citizens were mere subjects, and the "divine right of kings" was taken seriously. The very idea of a government of the people, by the people, and for the people seemed radical.

We can go back even earlier than the formal establishment of this nation. Columbus named the first land he discovered San Salvador (Holy Savior) and testified that he would never have found the land had he not been guided by his Savior and Lord.

The Mayflower Compact and the earliest documents organizing the colonies all acknowledged the sovereignty of Almighty God. Sure, the colonists had their differences, and they found comfort in being with others who shared their beliefs. Anglicans settled Virginia; Puritans, New England; Baptists, Pennsylvania; and Catholics, Maryland. But when the time came to decide whether to be loyal to the king of England or to become an independent country, representatives from all denominations who met in Williamsburg were united in their belief that this would be a God-fearing nation.

The Declaration of Independence based its principles on spiritual roots. "We hold these Truths to be self-evident, that all Men are created equal, and that they are endowed by their Creator with certain inalienable Rights." Each signer of the Declaration of Independence stood silently in a moment of prayer before affixing his signature to the document.

In George Washington's first inaugural address, he clearly stated the thinking of the earliest American citizens: "It would be peculiarly improper to omit in this first official act my fervent supplications to that Almighty Being who rules over the universe . . . that his benediction may consecrate to the liberties and happiness of the people of the United States a Government."

It's simply impossible to imagine the United States apart from its strong and deep spiritual heritage.

Our earliest citizens demanded the freedom to worship God as their consciences directed and were careful to guard that fundamental freedom. The late Richard Halverson, while he was chaplain of the U.S. Senate, put it in perspective: "The so-called 'separation of church and state' is not a license to ignore religion, but a testimony to its importance in our lives. Freedom *of* religion ought never be confused with freedom *from* religion."

John McCollister

INTRODUCTION

I have learned that Chester A. Arthur is one man
and the president of the United States is another.

—CHESTER A. ARTHUR
Twenty-first president of the United States

"So help me God."

They are just four innocent-sounding, monosyllabic words, but with them, forty-two men ceased for a time to be private citizens.

These four simple, prayerlike words were added, unexpectedly, to the prepared oath of office by General George Washington on April 30, 1789. They have been repeated by every successor, transforming each individual into a focal point of American history: president of the United States.

In a land without dictators or kings, these forty-two men have approached deification, for this is the only office in America in which the name of a person is guaranteed immortality. Every president knows who he is and, eventually, where he fits into history.

"So help me God."

From the moment he utters those four words, the new president begins to shape his history. Whatever he says or does is observed, monitored, and recorded by the press and then served up on a platter to an American public hungry for such news.

On one hand, we Americans pride ourselves as independent, self-determined individuals; on the other hand, we allow ourselves to be influenced by the so-called presidential patterns. Remember? President Kennedy disliked wearing hats, and our nation's hatters suffered a major setback. President Eisenhower rekindled an interest in golf. President Reagan made jelly beans fashionable.

We may look down our noses at the Hollywood gossip columnists, yet we perk up our ears for news about some facet of a president's personal life and habits—including his religious faith. If he attends church service, we want to know about it. If he doesn't attend, we want to know about that, too.

In a sense, it's a "no-win" situation for the president. If he seldom attends public worship, he's branded an infidel; if he's thought to attend too often, or applauds the efforts of some faith-based organization, he is accused of parading his religion.

Among the president's other Herculean burdens, it falls upon his shoulders to maintain a proper balance.

History is not an exact science, so it is not just a challenge, but a duty, for any writer to be as precise as possible in his or her presentation of the facts. Unfortunately, as any schoolchild knows, authors of history books often season their accounts with stories that are untrue. A youthful George Washington, for example, did not chop down the cherry tree. Also, there is no credible record to substantiate the image of a famous painting by Arnold Friberg that portrays a humble General Washington kneeling at Valley Forge in a solemn prayer for God's protection.

This author, therefore, reveals how these temporary residents of the eighteen-acre plot at 1600 Pennsylvania Avenue expressed the deepest of all human feelings—personal religious faith—in their *own* words, whenever possible.

Introduction

Throughout these accounts, one common note rings loud and clear: whatever any chief executive did or said became subject to public criticism.

Could it be that we Americans expect from our president a moral perfection impossible for the rest of us to attain?

GEORGE WASHINGTON (1722–1799)

State Born: Virginia   Occupation: Farmer

Party: Federalist   Religion: Deist (attended Episcopal)

GEORGE WASHINGTON

FIRST PRESIDENT

1789–1797

It is impossible to account for the creation of the universe,
without the agency of a Supreme Being. It is impossible to govern the universe,
without the aid of a Supreme Being. It is impossible to reason without
arriving at a Supreme Being.

—GEORGE WASHINGTON

He was the "macho man" of the eighteenth century.

Traditional historians may chafe at this description of our first president; although, were George Washington living today, he would be a leader of men, a heartthrob of ladies, and an idol of teenagers.

The story of every nation is peppered with examples of people who respond like hypnotized sheep to a personification of strength. This young nation was no exception. No American was ever so powerful in his era, nor perhaps in any other period of history, than the father of our country. His imposing stature for the era (six feet two inches tall, 175 pounds), coupled with his uncanny political savvy, made him the ideal candidate to weld the people.

GOD AND THE OVAL OFFICE

As commander of the Continental army, General George Washington succeeded in turning back the British chiefly because he was able to keep the military forces of the thirteen colonies united. Two days before the signing of the Declaration of Independence, on July 2, 1776, Washington rallied his troops for battle by declaring:

"The time is now near at hand which must probably determine whether Americans are to be freemen or slaves. . . . The fate of unborn millions will now depend, under God, on the courage and conduct of this army."

After the War for Independence, President George Washington had to reunite the citizens and transform them into "one nation under God."

Once the cord to Mother England was broken, the real problems for the Colonists began. Trust of one citizen for one another had long since waned. Inflation spiraled. International trade was disrupted. Coping with the newly won freedom was a greater hurdle than gaining it. Something, or someone, had to organize and direct the nation through the infant stage of an experiment called democracy.

The call went out, and George Washington was elected president by unanimous vote of the Electoral College.

One of Washington's officers, Henry "Light Horse Harry" Lee, summed up the feelings of the nation about its first president: "First in war, first in peace, and first in the hearts of his countrymen."

General Lee would have been less than honest were he to have added "first in his church." George Washington, whose rhetoric influenced the masses, did not talk openly about his religious heritage.

A CONSPICUOUS SILENCE

Washington was raised as an Anglican. He learned the Ten Commandments and the Apostles' Creed at the Truro Parish Church where his father was a vestryman. On Sunday mornings, he prayed, "Pardon, I beseech Thee, my sins; remove them from Thy presence, as far as the east is from the west, and accept me for the merits of Thy son, Jesus Christ." An Anglican clergyman performed the marriage ceremony for the not-yet twenty-seven-year-old Colonel Wash-ington to the widow Martha Dandridge Curtis at her home on January 6, 1759.

Washington maintained his association with the Anglican Church throughout his life, and worshiped on occasion at Christ Episcopal Church in Alexandria, Virginia. Nevertheless, as a result of his conspicuous silence in terms of any endorsement of the Episcopal faith, he was considered at least by some of his contemporaries to be a deist, an agnostic, even an atheist.

President Washington quite probably could have stifled this gossip with a strong statement about his Christian conviction. Certainly, the Christian community and its influential clergymen would have welcomed this. Yet the political climate of the eighteenth century was unique, and the new president was willing to act and speak within the boundaries set by the times for the sake of the country.

The embryonic nation was smarting from a war that many of its citizens chose not to endorse. Contrary to popular belief, not every able-bodied man rushed to the front for the chance to fire a musket at the English Redcoats. In reality, on April 19, 1775, when the Revolutionary War began with "the shot heard 'round the world," at least a fourth of the colonists supported England.

After four years of fighting and the surrender of the British at Yorktown, bitterness and hatred still seethed in America's own back-yards between Patriots and Loyalists. Tensions mounted daily. People lacked confidence in themselves and in the new nation. They groped for the right way and were eager to follow a leader who could give them a sense of direction. The battle was no longer with a foreign principality; now it was an internal strife marked with struggles for power that threatened the essential need for unity.

Where was the church in all of this? Unfortunately, it did little if anything to curb dissension. Perhaps both clergy and laypeople feared that a mingling of church and state would invite problems akin to those of other countries, in which the church became the main political force.

Meanwhile, some religious zealots added fuel to the existing fires of prejudice by crying out against "those foreign Catholics." Banners demanding No Popery flew in parts of New England. Many Protestant pastors preached sermons on the potential dangers of electing "papal loyalists" to public office. "Heaven help us," they warned, "if a Roman Catholic were to be elected president."

George Washington was well aware of this anti-Catholic frenzy. He knew, too, that religious persecution often generated civil wars and that the new nation could not survive another conflict. In his role as commander in chief and, again, as president of the United States, he insisted upon the uninhibited freedom of religious expression.

This was not a new quest for the dynamic leader. While serving as general of the Continental Army, Washington tried to curtail expressions of anti-Catholicism. He wrote numerous letters to denominational leaders of Baptist, Presbyterian, Methodist, Quaker, and Dutch Reformed churches asking for their help in promoting tolerance. "Religion and Morality are the essential pillars of Civil Society," he wrote. He urged them all to respect one another and to strive, as did he, to be "a faithful and impartial patron of genuine, vital religion."

In a letter written to a general convention of the Episcopal Church in 1789, Washington wrote, "The liberty enjoyed by the people of these States, of worshiping Almighty God agreeably to their consciences, is not only among the choices of their blessings, but also of their rights."

Mindful of his personal influence in such matters, George Washington was careful to avoid anything that hinted of partiality on his part, to the point that he even refused to partake of Holy Communion in the Episcopal Church once the American Revolution began. Consequently, his religious pronouncements and actions, which were broad in scope, caused some of his critics to question openly whether he was a Christian—using their definition of the term *Christian,* of course.

This is not to imply that President Washington was a "closet Christian" who smothered his real theology under a blanket of secrecy just to ensure unity among his people. Washington was diametrically opposed, for example, to the prevailing Calvinistic teaching that humans are sinners and must depend on the grace of Almighty God for any hope of salvation. Instead, he firmly believed in the ultimate goodness of people, a goodness that was, as he wrote in a letter dated May 26, 1789, "particularly necessary for advancing and confirming the happiness of our country."

A Surprising Expression of Faith

Every once in a while, without apparent reservation, George Washington exhibited an occasional spontaneous expression of religious faith. For instance, at his first inauguration on Thursday, April 30, 1789, with Vice President–elect John Adams and others, General George Washington walked out onto the balcony of Federal Hall on Wall Street in New York City to the sound of a thunderous ovation from the thousands of people—most of whom had waited for hours—jammed in the street below. The crowd suddenly became quiet as General Washington turned toward Judge Robert R. Livingston and placed his left hand on an opened Bible sitting upon a table beside him. He raised his right hand, and swore to "faithfully execute the office of the president of the United States." There was a

GOD AND THE OVAL OFFICE

pause. Then the president boldly added his own words: "I swear, so help me God."

A murmur rushed through the crowd and the inaugural party. This was not part of the oath of office (although every president, since, has adopted it). Washington then bent forward and kissed the Bible. Another murmur. Justice Livingston turned to the crowd below and cried out, "Long live George Washington, president of the United States!" The people cheered. Church bells pealed. Cannons at the fort fired a salute.

After a few moments, the president went inside to deliver his inaugural address, after which he and other officials were to ride in a carriage to St. Paul's Chapel on Broadway and Fulton Streets for a religious service. But, because most of the crowd remained on the streets, the president suggested that they walk the seven blocks to hear prayers offered by Episcopal bishop Samuel Provoost, who had just been named chaplain of the Senate. This was the only time a religious service was an official part of a presidential inauguration.

President George Washington was an unconventional man for an unconventional age. Although he was dearly loved by the people the *Philadelphia Journal* said in 1777, "Had he lived in the days of idolatry, he would have been worshiped as a god." Washington adopted an image unlike that of any national leader of his time. He was neither a dictator nor a monarch. He assumed, instead, a different kind of role—as protector and servant of the people. His chief obligation was not to himself but to the citizens of the United States. For him, as exemplified even through his religious expressions, personal wishes remained far down his list of priorities as compared to his obligations as president. The office, according to President Washington, was greater than the man filling it.

It was a legacy that, in years to come, would benefit some of his successors and prove to be the downfall of others.

6

HIGHLIGHTS OF THE ADMINISTRATION OF GEORGE WASHINGTON

- 1789—Judiciary Act specifies the number of federal courts and judges.

- 1790—Supreme Court meets for first time with John Jay as Chief Justice.

- 1790—Bill of Rights takes effect.

- 1790—Rhode Island, the last of the thirteen colonies, becomes a state.

- 1791—Vermont becomes a state.

- 1792—United States Post Office established as a separate entity.

- 1792—New York Stock Exchange is organized.

- 1793—War breaks out between Britain and France. The United States remains neutral.

- 1793—Washington elected to second term.

- 1794—Whiskey Rebellion begins.

- 1795—Pinckney's Treaty with Spain opens navigation of Mississippi River.

- 1796—Washington delivers his farewell address.

JOHN ADAMS (1735–1826)

State Born: Massachusetts   Occupation: Lawyer
Party: Federalist   Religion: Unitarian

JOHN ADAMS

SECOND PRESIDENT
1797–1801

*I have been a church-going animal for seventy-six years, and
this has been alleged as proof of my hypocrisy.*

—JOHN ADAMS
*August 28, 1811,
letter to Dr. Benjamin Rush*

Although John Adams was vice president for eight years, his name was not a household word. Due in part to President Washington's strong personality, Mr. Adams played only minor roles in the national political scene. Consequently, it was not until John Adams was elected president that people were curious about personal matters such as his faith.

"Ask me not whether I am Catholic or Protestant, Calvinistic or Armenian," Adams said. "As far as they are Christians, I wish to be a fellow disciple with them all."

HIS GROWING DOUBTS ABOUT CHRISTIANITY

Compared with the solid convictions of his predecessor, Adams's Christian testimony was woefully shallow. For one who had studied for the holy ministry during his college days, such a vague statement seemed out of character. However, during his study at Harvard, young Adams, under the instruction of the brilliant scientist Dr. John Winthrop, expressed growing doubts about his Christian convictions. It was not long before he felt "not made for the pulpit." Finally, he abandoned all thoughts of serving a parish, pursuing instead a degree in law. That decision led him into the political arena as a delegate to the First Continental Congress, member of the Massachusetts legislature, envoy to France and the Netherlands, minister to Great Britain, and first vice president of the United States.

John Adams was a scholarly man whose mastery of the language left no doubt as to where he stood on any issue. Nevertheless, it is difficult to compartmentalize his religious beliefs.

On one hand he admitted to his friend Dr. Benjamin Rush, "I have been a churchgoing animal for seventy-six years, and this has been alleged as proof of my hypocrisy." On the other hand, Adams was not a professing Christian; he was a Unitarian whose religious convictions allowed him to continue the quest for a unified nation begun by George Washington.

DISTRUST AMONG DENOMINATIONS

Most historians agree that one of the reasons for the successful unification of the new nation lay in the fact that each of its first four presidents, for all practical purposes, were deist (Washington, Jefferson, Madison) or Unitarian (Adams). Because of the distrust among the traditional denominations of the Christian church, the essential unity necessary for the survival of this infant nation would have never been realized had an ardent Baptist, Presbyterian, Methodist, or Dutch Reformed believer been elected as chief executive. In a nation of such religious diversity and fervor, neutrality in government was the only way to ensure peace on earth.

ADAMS'S DISTRUST OF DENOMINATIONS

John Adams certainly showed no partiality toward any of the conventional denominations. On the contrary, he more often chided the mainline churches for their unwillingness to rise from the mire of outdated teachings. He once asked his friend John Taylor in a letter dated 1814:

> Even since the Reformation, when or where has existed a Protestant or dissenting sect who would tolerate iniquity? The blackest billingsgate, the most ungentlemanly insolence, the most yahooish brutality is patiently endured, countenanced, propagated, and applauded. But touch a solemn truth in collision with a dogma or sect, though capable of the clearest proof, and you will soon find you have disturbed a nest, and the hornets will swarm about your legs and hands and fly into your face and eyes.

At times, however, John Adams spoke and wrote as though he was at least sympathetic toward the beliefs of mainline Christians. This eldest son of a church deacon once described Christianity as "the brightest of the glory and the express portrait of the character of the eternal, self-existent, independent, benevolent, all powerful, and all merciful creator, preserver, and father of the universe, the first good, and first fair."

On December 27, 1816, Adams wrote, "Jesus is benevolence personified, an example for all men."

In one of his diary entries, he describes the Christian religion as "above all the religions that previously existed in ancient or modern times, the religion of virtue, equity and humanity. It is resignation to God, it is goodness itself to man."

COURTSHIP AND MARRIAGE

America's struggle for freedom occupied Adams's waking hours. Courtship and marriage fell far down his list of priorities, until one day, he met a spirited seventeen-year-old who was reading John Locke's *Human Understanding*, an exceptionally challenging bit of philosophy.

"My, what a big book for such a little head," he observed.

Without so much as looking up, Abigail Smith replied, "Even a little head longs for knowledge."

"Then what do you see as our purpose on earth?" asked Adams.

The clergyman's daughter answered pointedly, "Men and women are here to serve God and humanity. We are accountable to God for every moment of our time. We are made in the image of God, and we must fulfill our promise or we are a blasphemy to God. An hour wasted is an hour's sin."

Her intellect and devotion won his heart. They were married three years later on October 25, 1764. The union bore them five children.

During their fifty-four years of marriage (which he himself described as a "love feast"), Adams often said of his wife: "She makes me so happy! No sour-faced girl who makes everyone feel sad, her Christian beliefs make her ever a joy to know."

FIRST TO OCCUPY THE WHITE HOUSE

John Adams, who served one term, was the first chief executive to live in the White House. It might be said that it was he who left the most noticeable mark of his religious conviction as a guideline for each of the occupants who followed. Above the fireplace in the president's formal dining room is inscribed the prayer written by the nation's second president:

> *I Pray Heaven to Bestow*
> *the Best of Blessings on*
> *THIS HOUSE*
> *and on All that shall hereafter*
> *Inhabit it. May none but Honest*
> *and Wise Men ever rule under this Roof!*

After his defeat for reelection by Thomas Jefferson in 1800, John Adams retired from public life to study history, philosophy, and religion. Through a strange twist of fate, both of these former presidents died on July 4, 1826—the fiftieth anniversary of America's independence.

HIGHLIGHTS OF THE
ADMINISTRATION OF JOHN ADAMS

- 1796—Tennessee becomes a state.
- 1796—*E Pluribus Unum* ("Out of many, one") is added to American coins.
- 1797—America is almost brought to war by the "XYZ Affair."
- 1800—United States capital moves from Philadelphia to Washington, D.C.
- 1800—Library of Congress is established.
- 1800—Adams loses bid for reelection to Thomas Jefferson.

THOMAS JEFFERSON (1743–1826)

State Born: Virginia   Occupation: Planter/Lawyer

Party: Democrat   Religion: Deist

THOMAS JEFFERSON

THIRD PRESIDENT

1801–1809

*I have sworn on the altar of God eternal hostility
against every form of tyranny of the mind of men.*

—THOMAS JEFFERSON,
during the presidential campaign of 1800

Wh!hen John F. Kennedy was president of the United States, he
hosted a formal White House dinner in 1962 honoring the winners
of the Nobel Peace Prize. Prior to the serving of the meal, the president remarked, "This is probably the greatest concentration of talent
and genius in this house except for perhaps those times when
Thomas Jefferson ate alone."

Indeed, no student of American history will doubt that Thomas
Jefferson was one of the more gifted people ever elected as chief executive of these United States. Jefferson was an accomplished man in
many arenas.

Perhaps Thomas Jefferson's refusal to identify with any specific denomination or creed lay in the fact that he had such a wide range of interests that he refused to be confined to just one way of looking at things—including religion.

A RENAISSANCE MAN

Thomas Jefferson was one of our country's true Renaissance men. The Virginian's political accomplishments are widely known: author of the Declaration of Independence, member of the Continental Congress and the Virginia House of Delegates, governor of Virginia, secretary of state under Washington, vice president under John Adams, and president for two terms.

He was preeminent in other fields as well. He designed Monticello, along with other buildings in Virginia, and became known as the father of our national architecture. Jefferson was also the first major American art collector; he was president of the American Philosophical Society (which then meant scientific speculation and investigation); he was a genuine scholar, with more than a cursory knowledge of Greek, Latin, French, Italian, and Spanish; he was the first American statesman to foster public education; and he was the founder of the University of Virginia. At the College of William and Mary, Jefferson studied law with Professor George Wythe from 1760 to 1762. He was admitted to the bar five years later.

Into every generation comes someone who embodies the word *genius*. Thomas Jefferson was one of those people. Respected historians such as Dr. Hilmar Grimm, professor emeritus of Ohio's Capital University, claim that part of Jefferson's genius lay in his ability to see beyond the moment. He could have gained political strength by aligning with any of the traditional churches of his day.

But of more importance to him was providing an opportunity for thinking men and women to structure their own beliefs—and fate.

POLITICAL AMBITIONS OF A RUMORED ATHEIST

During the campaign of 1800, Jefferson was vilified variously as a deist, atheist, and agnostic. As late as 1830, the Philadelphia Public Library refused to place his writing on its shelves, calling him an infidel. Actually, Jefferson was not an infidel—"of no faith." Instead, he held to a different faith. "Say nothing about my religion," he admonished a friend. "It is known to my God and myself, alone."

Although he did not affiliate with any Christian denomination, Jefferson occasionally patronized the organized church. During his years as president, for instance, he frequently worshiped with the congregation of Christ Episcopal Church, which met for services in a small, wooden, abandoned tobacco warehouse at New Jersey Avenue and B Street SE, below Capitol Hill.

One Sunday morning, as Jefferson was crossing an open field near the Capitol, a large, red prayer book under his left arm, a stranger stopped him and asked where he was going.

"To church," Jefferson replied.

The man burst out laughing and said, "Why, Mr. President, you don't believe a word of it."

"Sir," Jefferson answered, "no nation has yet existed or been governed without religion. I, as the chief magistrate of this nation, am bound to give it the sanction of my example. Good morning, sir." And he marched off as the stranger, open-mouthed, gazed at him.

On every New Year's Day, he sent a note with fifty dollars to the rector, the Reverend Andrew J. McCormick.

Some historians insist on squeezing Jefferson into the mold of traditional Christianity, but to do so would serve as an injustice to everything Jefferson believed.

EARLY INFLUENCE BY DEISTS

Jefferson's religious views generally echoed eighteenth-century deism, which we might equate with modern-day Unitarianism, rather than with those of mainline Christian denominations. Yet much of his early education was Christian oriented. His parents, Peter and Jane Jefferson of Albemarle County, Virginia, were devout Anglicans. When he was only nine years old, Jefferson went to live with the Reverend Douglas A. Scott, a dedicated Calvinist, who taught the young Jefferson Latin, Greek, and French. He attended a school run by the Reverend James Maury, a descendent of the Huguenots, in nearby Charlottesville.

But it was as a college student at William and Mary that Jefferson shaped his thinking about humankind and God. It was here, Jefferson confessed, "I got my first views of the expansion of science and of the system of things in which we are placed."

During his college days, Thomas Jefferson showed signs of distrusting organized religion. He had a growing conviction that clergymen were corrupting the pure and simple message of Jesus.

Our third president was sensitive to the charge that he was opposed to the teachings of Christianity. In a letter to his friend, Benjamin Rush, Jefferson asserted his religious beliefs as being

the result of a life in inquiry and reflection and . . . very different from the anti-Christian system attributed to me by those who know nothing of my opinions. To the corruptions of Christianity I am indeed opposed, but not to genuine precepts of Jesus himself. I am a Christian, but I am a Christian in the only sense in which I believe Jesus wished anyone to be, sincerely attached to his doctrine in preference to all others, ascribing to him all human excellence, and believing that he never claimed any other.

Thomas Jefferson

The "Jefferson Bible"

Thomas Jefferson considered himself a disciple of Jesus, although not in the sense endorsed by most of the clergy of his day. While he abstained from what most clergymen deemed to be vices—using tobacco, playing cards, and gambling—he did not accept the deity of Jesus, a fundamental dogma of Christianity. Nonetheless, he admired the simple teachings of Jesus.

In 1815 he published a compilation of Jesus's quotes into a small volume containing passages from the four Gospels. He titled his work *The Life and Morals of Jesus of Nazareth.* Today it's often referred to simply as *The Jefferson Bible.* To compile his version of the Bible, Jefferson took a pair of scissors and snipped away all the letters of St. Paul and eliminated any reports about the miracles of Jesus or of any of the so-called supernatural aspects of Jesus's life, including his resurrection.

Jefferson claimed that this was his attempt "to separate the gold from the dross, restore to him the former, and leave the latter to the stupidity of some and the rouguery of others of his disciples."

Jefferson, who started compiling this book using verses written in Greek, Latin, French, and English, wrote his old friend Charles Thomson telling him how it came into existence:

I have made a wee little book which I call the philosophy of Jesus. It is the paradigm of his doctrines, made by cutting the texts out of the book and arranging them on the pages of a blank book, in a certain order of time and subject.

A more beautiful or precious morsel of ethics I have never seen. It is a document in proof that I am a *real Christian* (underlined by Jefferson in the original), that is to say, a disciple of the doctrines of Jesus.

The sometimes caustic Jefferson believed that Jesus's straight-forward teachings had been corrupted over the years by his devoted followers. In an 1820 letter to William Short, Jefferson left no doubt about his feelings when he referred to Paul as "the first corrupter of the doctrines of Jesus."

Jefferson's desire for the simple teachings of Jesus reflected his attitude about such things as worship. Jefferson did not seem comfortable in cathedrals. Instead, he felt religion was "a concern purely between God and our consciences." He shaped his personal theology through a set of rather rigid principles, as would Aristotle or any of the other ancient philosophers who were his heroes. Those principles showed little patience toward anyone who would prohibit freedom of thought or conscience. "I will never by any word or act," he promised, "bow to the shrine of intolerance or admit the right of inquiry into the religious opinions of others."

IMPORTANCE OF RELIGIOUS FREEDOM

In Jefferson's home state of Virginia, for example, the Anglican Church enjoyed such a strong influence that other denominations were hard-pressed to survive. Jefferson strongly objected to this preferred status. Hence, he sponsored a bill for religious freedom that said, in part, "No man shall be compelled to frequent or support any religious worship, place, or ministry whatsoever . . . but all men shall be free to profess, and by argument to maintain, their opinions in matters of religion."

Jefferson's religion was a subjective, personal relationship with the Creator. "There is only one God, and He is all perfect," he wrote, "and to love God with all thy heart and thy neighbor as yourself is the sum of religion."

Perhaps this is why Jefferson did not consider his role as president of the United States as his top achievement. He showed what he deemed important when he wrote the epitaph that marks his grave at Monticello:

Author of the Declaration of Independence,
of the Statute of Virginia for Religious
Freedom, and Father of the
University of Virginia.

HIGHLIGHTS OF THE ADMINISTRATION OF THOMAS JEFFERSON

- 1803—Louisiana Territory is purchased from France for $15 million (approximately three cents per acre).

- 1803—Ohio becomes a state.

- 1804—Jefferson is reelected.

- 1804–1806—The Lewis and Clark expedition takes place.

- 1807—Embargo Act prohibits American exports.

JAMES MADISON (1751–1836)

State Born: Virginia   Occupation: Lawyer

Party: Democrat-Republican   Religion: Episcopal

JAMES MADISON

FOURTH PRESIDENT

1809–1817

In the Papal System (Roman Catholic), Government and Religion are in a manner consolidated, and that is found to be the worst of Government.

—JAMES MADISON, 1832

He was too small to make the team. As a schoolboy in Port Conway, Virginia, young James Madison could not compete successfully in events that required athletic prowess. The young man who would have the dubious distinction of becoming our shortest president (he stood five feet four inches tall and weighed less than one hundred pounds) sought, instead, to make his mark in life through the tamer arena of academics, which included some formal study of the Bible and other religious teachings.

After earning a B.A. degree from Princeton in 1771, this diminutive youth, whom Washington Irving described as "a withered little apple-johnny," remained on campus for another year studying theology, Hebrew, and law, and he seriously considered the idea of entering the holy ministry. Although this thought was short-lived, Mr. Madison read books on theology just for relaxation, a practice that he continued throughout his adult life.

ANGLICAN ROOTS

As was the case with most of the youngsters raised in colonial Virginia, Madison was schooled in the teachings of the Anglican Church. At the same time, even while he was a student, he insisted strongly on a separation of church and state, something that he vigorously supported when he helped frame the Constitution of the United States.

EFFORTS TO SEPARATE RELIGION AND GOVERNMENT

Carrying his conviction to its logical conclusion, Madison was one of the few elected officials who opposed the establishment of a chaplain for the Congress. In 1811, as president, he vetoed an act of incorporation of the Episcopal Church in the District of Columbia. He felt that such an intrusion violated the Constitution's First Amendment regarding the establishment of religion.

In the Bill of Rights for the State of Virginia, of which Madison was the primary author, he wrote "Religion, or the duty we owe our Creator, and the manner of discharging it, can be directed only by reason and conviction, not by force or violence; and, therefore, all men are equally entitled to the free exercise of religion according to the dictates of conscience."

However, Madison studied theology and, on occasion, acknowledged the presence of Almighty God. In his first inaugural address in 1809, he confessed that the power of Almighty God "regulates the destiny of nations." Yet his cousin, Episcopal bishop James Madison, observed, "His religious feelings died a quick death."

Like his predecessor and personal idol, Thomas Jefferson, Madison remained silent concerning his opinions about established religion, and he and his wife, Dolly, a Quaker, periodically attended worship services at St. John's Episcopal Church in Washington. His only genuine interest in the organized church, it seems, surfaced when some issue threatened the separation of church and state. Then, he became so outspoken on this point that the more conservative Calvinists of his day concluded that the president was "anti-church."

DISCRIMINATION AMONG DENOMINATIONS

Perhaps the underlying reason for his constant hammering away on this theme lay in the fact that Madison was raised in an environment of sophisticated Virginians who supported only the Anglican tradition and openly discriminated against Baptist, Presbyterian, and Congregationalist fellowships through fines, imprisonments, and banishments. This, he felt, was a sacrilege.

Once, when Patrick Henry introduced legislation to tax the public for the support of religious teaching, Madison retorted, "If this freedom be abused, it is an offense against God, not against men. To God, therefore, not to man, must an account be rendered." As a postscript, he added, "In this country is forever extinguished the ambitious hope of making laws for the human mind."

President James Madison was not a staunch, churchgoing Christian to be sure. But he did all he could to ensure that others could be, if they wished it.

HIGHLIGHTS OF THE ADMINISTRATION OF JAMES MADISON

- 1812—Louisiana becomes a state.
- 1812—War is declared on England.

- 1813—Madison is reelected for a second term.
- 1814—The British capture and burn Washington, D.C.
- 1814—Treaty of Ghent ends War of 1812.
- 1816—Indiana becomes a state.

JAMES MONROE (1756–1831)

State Born: Virginia   Occupation: Lawyer

Party: Democrat-Republican   Religion: Episcopal

JAMES MONROE

FIFTH PRESIDENT

1817–1825

When we view the blessings with which our country has been favored, those which we now enjoy, and the means which we possess of handing them down unimpaired to our latest posterity, our attention is irresistably drawn to the source from whence they flow. Let us, then, unite in offering our most grateful acknowledgments for these blessings to the Divine Author of All Good.

—JAMES MONROE,
from his second annual message to Congress

The religious conviction of President James Monroe is best classified as "decision by indecision." His public religious observance, his marriage, and his funeral all took place in the Episcopal Church. No records offer any evidence that Mr. Monroe rejected the Anglican faith; at the same time, we have no record that he endorsed it, either.

As indicated by his lopsided victories in 1816 and again in 1820, James Monroe reflected the feelings of the nation. In a message to Congress in December 1823, he presented what is known as the "Monroe Doctrine" that forbade any European nation from extending its holdings or to use armed force on the two American continents. The doctrine has been a keystone of American foreign policy since then. The Revolutionary War was history, and the country wanted to settle down, relax, and grow a bit. Monroe was the ideal candidate. He didn't rock the boat. He did his job without any great fanfare, and maintained this attitude in terms of his personal faith, never trumpeting his religious convictions.

His Conspicuous Silence about Religion

Although President Monroe attended St. John's Episcopal Church in Washington during his two terms in office, he was conspicuous by his silence about his religious beliefs. "Religion," he said, "is a matter between our Maker and ourselves." As a result, aside from occasional passing references in his formal speeches—including both inaugural addresses—he seldom mentioned the Lord at all.

A longtime friend of President Monroe, Judge E. R. Watson of Virginia, thought of him as a good man because, as he put it, "I never hear him use an oath or utter a word of profanity."

Even the judge had to rule solely on the basis of lack of evidence.

HIGHLIGHTS OF THE ADMINISTRATION OF JAMES MONROE

- 1817—Mississippi becomes a state.

- 1818—Congress fixes the number of stripes on the United States flag at thirteen to honor the original colonies, and stars to be added with each new state.

- 1818—Anglo-American Convention sets the 49th parallel as the border separating the United States and Canada.

- 1818—Illinois becomes a state.

- 1819—Florida cedes from Spain to become part of the United States in exchange for $5 million in cancelled Spanish debts.

- 1819—Alabama becomes a state.

- 1820—Missouri Compromise forbids slavery in America above 36 degrees, 30 minutes latitude.

- 1820—Maine becomes a state.

- 1820—Monroe is reelected for a second term.

- 1820—Monroe Doctrine is delivered to Congress.

- 1821—Missouri becomes a state.

JOHN QUINCY ADAMS (1767–1848)

State Born: Massachusetts   Occupation: Lawyer

Party: Democrat–Republican   Religion: Unitarian

JOHN QUINCY ADAMS

SIXTH PRESIDENT

1825–1829

I have made it a practice for several years
to read the Bible through in the course of every year.

—JOHN QUINCY ADAMS
in his diary, September 26, 1848

Like Father, like son. Because John Quincy Adams also expressed his religious beliefs in different words, some members of the organized church branded him as an atheist. He thereby received from his political enemies many of the same slings and arrows as did his father, our second president. Yet this did not appear to cause anxiety, for, like that of his father, John Quincy Adams's faith was strictly a personal relationship between himself and his God.

This was no lame excuse. Throughout his life, Adams maintained a practice of reading at least three chapters of the Bible each day. The astute Ralph Waldo Emerson observed many years later, "No man could read the Bible with such powerful effect, even with the cracked and winded voice of old age."

Like his father, John Quincy Adams was not a very large man (he was five feet seven inches), so he devoted himself to academic pursuits, studying poetry (he published a book of poems in 1831), the writings of Shakespeare, the classics, and the Bible.

In spite of his obvious love of Holy Scripture, we have no record that a Bible was used when he took his oath of office on March 4, 1825. If this is true, then John Quincy was the only president not to use one. However, in his inaugural address, he did conclude by quoting from Psalm 127: "knowing that 'except the LORD keep the city, the watchman waketh but in vain,' with fervent supplications for His favor, to His overruling providence I commit with humble but fearless confidence my own fate and the future destinies of my country."

ATTENDANCE AT CHURCH

As to attendance at public worship, it's safe to conclude that this was not always one of Adams's practices. While serving as secretary of state, he wrote about this fact in his diary entry of October 24, 1819. "Since I have now resided in Washington, I have not regularly attended at any church. . . . chiefly because, although the churches here are numerous and diversified, not one is of the Independent Congregational class to which I belong, the church to which I was bred, and in which I will die."

Later, however, Adams changed his approach. Frank E. Edington, historian of Washington's New York Avenue Presbyterian Church, records that while Adams was president, he served as a trustee and attended worship there more often than many of those on the membership rolls. On several occasions, according to

Edington, the president loaned substantial sums of money to the congregation in order to defray current bills.

An Unhappy Presidency

"I can scarcely conceive a more harassing, wearying, teasing condition of existence," John Quincy Adams said.

Consequently, some of his rare moments of contentment were found while sitting inside a church. "Hope in the goodness of God, reliance upon His mercy in affliction, trust in Him to bring light out of darkness and good out of evil are the comforts and promises which I desire from public worship," he said. "They help to sustain me in the troubles that are thickening around me."

Adams was not what you would call a popular president. Often setting principle above party, he spoke out strongly about controversial issues such as slavery. Pro-slavery forces called him "the madman from Massachusetts." Eventually, he made so many enemies, it cost him his bid for reelection in 1828.

His Continued Fight Against Slavery

Two years later, however, Adams returned to the nation's capital as a representative of his neighbors of Braintree (now Quincy), Massachusetts, and he used the political platform for seventeen years as his sounding board against slavery. His polished speeches earned him a more respected title: "Old Man Eloquent."

In this fight, one thing disappointed him the most. Adams saw in the organized churches the potential to challenge and eventually curb the growing evils of slavery. He lamented the fact that neither the clergymen nor their flocks did much to rid society of this plague. In a pointed letter of May 27, 1838, he wrote:

The counterfeit character of a very large portion of the Christian ministry of this country is disclosed in the dissensions growing up in all the Protestant churches on the subject of slavery. This question of slavery is convulsing the Congregational churches in Massachusetts; it is deeply agitating the Methodists; it has already completed a schism in the Presbyterian Church.

He spoke his mind; he made enemies. Nevertheless, he was able to maintain respect even from the opposition. Upon hearing of Adams's death in 1843, political rival Martin Van Buren said of him, "He was an honest man, not only incorruptible himself, but an enemy to corruption everywhere."

"The slave has lost a champion," said clergyman Theodore Parker. "America has lost a supporter, and freedom has lost an unfailing friend."

In an appropriate farewell, the Reverend William Lunt based his funeral sermon on the famous passage from Revelation 2:10: "Be thou faithful unto death, and I will give thee a crown of life."

Life father, like son.

HIGHLIGHTS OF THE ADMINISTRATION OF JOHN QUINCY ADAMS

- 1825—Henry Clay is appointed as secretary of state.

- 1825—The Erie Canal is completed.

- 1828—Adams is defeated in his bid for reelection by Andrew Jackson.

ANDREW JACKSON (1767–1845)

State Born: South Carolina   Occupation: Lawyer/Soldier

Party: Democrat   Religion: Presbyterian

ANDREW JACKSON

SEVENTH PRESIDENT

1829–1837

First, I bequeath my body to the dust whence it comes, and my soul to God who gave it, hoping for a happy immortality through the atoning merits of our Lord Jesus Christ, the Saviour of the world.

—ANDREW JACKSON,
preamble of his last will and testament

His nickname was "Old Hickory," and that wasn't by chance. The gruff, military hero who became our nation's seventh president spurned the conventional formalities of his day, while standing for principle.

After he had established himself as a successful attorney in Nashville, Tennessee, Andrew Jackson met and fell in love with Rachel, the daughter of Colonel John Donelson. Rachel was in the process of acquiring a divorce. Once the divorce was finalized (or so they thought), the two became husband and wife in August 1791. Due to a technicality, however, Rachel's divorce was not legal. Once this technicality was satisfied two years later, they were quietly remarried in Nashville.

The Toll of Gossip

Jackson's political enemies, nevertheless, in an attempt to discredit him, delighted in repeating juicy stories about his wife, "the bigamist." Jackson even fought duels in defense of her honor, but he could not still the whispers of the Washington gossips.

Though Jackson was able to override the rumors and win the presidential election, strain of the campaign and the scandal took its toll. Rachel Jackson suffered a heart attack and died, one week before Inauguration Day.

According to biographer Marquis James, the most difficult thing for "Old Hickory" to say was that he had forgiven his enemies. "He made it clear," said James, "that only *his* enemies were absolved. Those who slandered Rachel remained for God to deal with."

An Undying Love

Clement Conger, former curator of the White House, revealed that President Jackson carried with him a locket containing a miniature portrait of his departed wife. At night, he would open that locket and place it on the table beside his bed so that it would be the last thing he would see before falling asleep and the first thing he would see upon awakening in the morning. Today, a painting inspired by that picture in the locket hangs in the lower East Wing of the White House.

Before her untimely death, Rachel Jackson and her husband worshiped together at a Presbyterian Church. As a result, several weeks after she died, the president fulfilled a promise to her by uniting with a small Presbyterian congregation located near his home, the Hermitage.

A New Scandal

Scandal remained a part of President Jackson's career, however. Shortly after he entered office, Jackson embarked on another crusade, defending a lady with a "tarnished reputation." Young Peggy O'Neal, the daughter of a Washington innkeeper, married Secretary of War Eaton. But, because of her alleged past indiscretions, she never was accepted by Washington society, especially by the wives of some of the other cabinet members.

Some of the gossip was repeated by the young Reverend John N. Campbell, pastor of the Second Presbyterian Church, which the president attended faithfully while in office. When he heard of Pastor Campbell's contribution to the rumor mill, President Jackson, according to Pulitzer Prize historian, Constance McLaughlin Green, summoned the minister to the White House and gave him "a stinging rebuke for maligning a pure and innocent woman." That afternoon, the president severed all relationships with that congregation.

HIS LOVE OF SCRIPTURE REMAINED

Beneath his rough edges and hair-trigger temper, the man who once said, "I have only two regrets—that I have not shot Henry Clay or hanged John C. Calhoun," had a deep appreciation for Holy Scripture. In his diary, he recorded that it was his custom to read three to five chapters from the Bible each day. He wrote to one of his sons-in-law, "Go read the Scriptures, the joyful promises it contains will be a balsam to all your troubles."

He had troubles, just as did every other occupant of the White House. Yet until his dying day, President Jackson maintained a staunch faith that matched his zeal for living.

On March 24, 1845, a friend, William Yack, recalled that the seventy-nine-year-old former president knew death was but a short time away. After taking Holy Communion in the presence of his family, the weakened warrior turned to them and said, "Death has no terror for me. . . . What are my sufferings compared to those of the blessed Saviour? I am ready to depart when called."

As his family gathered at his bedside on June 8, 1845, Jackson uttered his farewell. "Do not cry," he said. "Be good children, and we shall all meet in heaven."

HIGHLIGHTS OF THE ADMINISTRATION OF ANDREW JACKSON

- 1829—Jackson gives government jobs to 2,000 supporters.

- 1830—Jackson signs the Indian Removal Act.

- 1832—Jackson is reelected to second term.

- 1832—The attempt to recharter the Second Bank of the United States is vetoed, which leads to the creation of the Whig Party.

- 1832—Federal troops are sent to South Carolina when the state attempted to nullify Federal Tariff Laws.

- 1835—The United States is debt-free for the only time in its history.

- 1836—Mexican troops defeat Texans at the Alamo.

- 1836—Gold and silver deemed only currency acceptable to purchase federal lands.

- 1836—Arkansas becomes a state.

MARTIN VAN BUREN (1782–1862)

State Born: New York   Occupation: Lawyer

Party: Democrat   Religion: Reformed

MARTIN
VAN BUREN

EIGHTH PRESIDENT
1837–1841

I only look to the gracious protection of the Divine Being whose strengthening support I humbly solicit and to whom I fervently pray to look down upon us all.

—MARTIN VAN BUREN

On Sundays in Kinderhook, New York, around the turn of the nineteenth century, churchgoers at the town's little Dutch Reformed Church included a small man with striking blond hair. Everyone knew when this man was in attendance. During the singing of hymns, his voice carried above the rest, especially when that hymn was "O God, Our Help in Ages Past"—his favorite.

The man with the booming voice was Martin Van Buren, who, along with his family, made public worship a regular weekly habit, even after he became the eighth president of the United States.

RELIGION AND POLITICS

President Van Buren's religious teachings and attitudes resulted from a long family tradition. Deeply ingrained in the Dutch Reformed Church, he was dismayed at the lack of any representative church in Washington, D.C. As a compromise, he became a regular worshiper—always using a special pew—at St. John's Episcopal Church. On occasion, he attended the New York Avenue Presbyterian Church located across the street from the White House.

Van Buren certainly knew that religious conviction had its political impact. Early in his career, while promoting the campaign of Andrew Jackson, Van Buren asked reporters, "Does the old gentleman have prayers in his house? If so, be sure to mention it, modestly, of course."

THE LITTLE MAGICIAN

The five-foot-six-inch Van Buren was nicknamed "Little Magician" because he was small in stature and able to do so much with so little. "'Tis only by the grace of God," he insisted.

Van Buren's inaugural address struck the same note. "I only look to the gracious protection of the Divine Being whose strengthening support I humbly solicit and to whom I fervently pray to look down upon us all."

The president—the first one born after the United States became an official nation—carried this attitude not only in victory, but also in defeat. When he lost his bid for reelection to William Henry Harrison in 1840, Van Buren called upon his victorious opponent to wish him God's richest blessings.

Two issues led to his failure to win a second term: his outspoken rhetoric against the expansion of slavery within the nation, and a massive depression generated by the collapse of many banks throughout the land.

In retirement, Van Buren continued to speak out against the evils of slavery and other social ills, but he had lost nearly all of his political clout.

In Van Buren's last years, the residents of Kinderhook waved to their most famous neighbor as he rode a carriage to church each Sunday. When he died on July 24, 1862, the congregation gathered to pay their final respects and to join together in singing, in his honor, "O God, Our Help in Ages Past."

HIGHLIGHTS OF THE ADMINISTRATION OF MARTIN VAN BUREN

- 1837—Michigan becomes a state.
- 1837—Banks close in New York City and Philadelphia, leading to a four-year depression.
- 1838—So-called Trail of Tears forces thousands of American Indians from their homes.
- 1840—Van Buren is defeated in his bid for reelection by William Henry Harrison.

WILLIAM HENRY HARRISON (1773–1841)

State Born: Virginia   Occupation: Farmer/Soldier

Party: Whig   Religion: Unaffiliated

                              (attended Episcopal)

WILLIAM HENRY HARRISON

NINTH PRESIDENT
1841

At first, reading it [the Bible] was a duty.
Now, it's a pleasure.

—WILLIAM HENRY HARRISON

On November 7, 1811, he won the battle against the Shawnee chief, Tecumseh, at the Tippecanoe River. He was a national hero who was swept into office, first as a senator and later as the president, perhaps remembered best for his campaign slogan: "Tippecanoe and Tyler too."

BRIEF TERM IN OFFICE

After all, what can be said about a president who served only one month in office? Very little. Yet this is quite possibly more than can be said about the outward signs of religious conviction displayed by William Henry Harrison.

Tradition records that Harrison was baptized an Episcopalian, although no official record exists to confirm this. While in Washington, he occasionally attended services and occupied pew number 45 at St. John's Episcopal Church, across Lafayette Square.

Once, when in Pittsburgh, Pennsylvania, the then president-elect was seen in his hotel room reading a Bible. The April 13, 1841, edition of the *National Intelligencer* reported Harrison explaining that this was a fixed habit of his for twenty years. "At first," he said, "it was a matter of duty. It has now become a pleasure."

SUDDEN DEATH

Perhaps in an effort to demonstrate his vigor at sixty-eight years of age, Harrison elected to wear no hat or coat on that cold, blustery March 4, 1841, while riding a horse in his inaugural parade. In addition, he delivered a long (one-hour, forty-five-minute) inaugural address outdoors. Since he studied medicine as a young man, he certainly should have been able to predict the consequences of his gesture. The president caught a cold that developed into pneumonia. On April 4, 1841, only one month after his inauguration, the president lay in bed, growing weaker by the moment. He asked a nurse to read aloud to him the Psalm 103: "Bless the Lord, O my soul, and all that is within me, bless his holy name."

A few minutes after the reading, the president closed his eyes and died peacefully.

At the Episcopal funeral service in the White House, the Reverend William Hawley, rector of St. John's Episcopal Church, stated that the day after his inauguration, the president purchased a Bible and a prayer book. Reverend Hawley held high the two books in view of the mourners, and he announced that the president never began a day without reading from both. Also, the minister declared that it was the president's desire to join in full communion with the church on the ensuing Easter Sunday. Neither story, however, is substantiated through any other source.

Was Reverend Hawley speaking the truth? Perhaps. Yet one thing is certainly true: William Henry Harrison was the first American president to die in office.

Old Tippecanoe had fought his last battle.

HIGHLIGHTS OF THE ADMINISTRATION OF WILLIAM HENRY HARRISON

- 1841—Harrison delivers the longest inaugural address in history—105 minutes. He dies one month later.

JOHN TYLER (1790–1862)

State Born: Virginia   Occupation: Lawyer

Party: Whig   Religion: Episcopal

JOHN
TYLER

TENTH PRESIDENT
1841–1845

*Nothing but the kind providence of our heavenly Father
could have saved me.*

—JOHN TYLER,
following his recovery from a serious illness

George Washington was the father of our country, but President John Tyler was the father of the White House. Our tenth president had fifteen children by two wives. He and Letitia Christian produced eight; after Letitia's death, Julia Gardiner (he was fifty-five years old and she was twenty-four at their marriage) bore him seven.

AN UNEXPECTED PRESIDENCY

John Tyler, normally, is remembered not for his personal efforts to increase the nation's population, but as being the first vice president to assume the duties of president. As such, he had his struggles with the

Constitution. Did the unexpected death of President Harrison mean that John Tyler was the president, or was he only, as the Constitution states, the one who would "act as president"?

His political enemies took delight in heaping sarcastic remarks on him for his newly acquired position. "Mr. Tyler, who styles himself the president of the United States" was one of the barbs thrown in his direction by former president John Quincy Adams, for example.

In spite of this, President Tyler was able to ward off the ridicule mustered by his foes with a calm reserve that matched the biblical admonition from Jesus's Sermon on the Mount, which he learned as a young lad in Charles City County, Virginia: "Love your enemies. Bless those who persecute you."

A Paradox

Tyler's life was punctuated by paradox. For instance, in terms of the moral issues surrounding slavery, he was openly a slaveholder who owned a labor force of seventy-five slaves on his twelve-hundred-acre plantation, Sherwood Forest, in Virginia. At the same time, as president he openly fought for emancipation. He said that the sight of slaves being bought and sold in public made him physically ill.

His life was a contrast even in terms of loyalty to the federal government. When he took the oath of office on April 6, 1841, he swore on an open Bible to "preserve, protect, and defend the Constitution of the United States," and while in office, took a strong stand against the secession of the South. Yet after leaving the White House, he was elected to the Confederate Congress and fought for the secession of the South.

On these, as well as other important issues, John Tyler made enemies in both camps. In describing the slender, six-foot president, astute author Charles Dickens wrote, "He looked somewhat worn and anxious, and well he might be, being at war with everybody."

STRONG CHRISTIAN CONVICTION

Behind all of this outward confusion lay a solid Christian conviction. "My life has always been illuminated by a bright faith in the Christian religion," Tyler said. Henry Wise, former governor of Virginia and close personal friend, remembered the tenth president as "a firm believer in the atonement of the Son of God and in the efficacy of his blood to wash away every stain of mortal sin. He was by faith and heirship a member of the Episcopal Church, and he never doubted divine revelation."

In retrospect, the presidential years were not kind to John Tyler. Outside of the annexation of Texas, no major accomplishment can be set in type for the history books. Since his track record was not sufficient to provide as much as a good campaign slogan, Tyler was rejected by his own party for renomination in 1844.

When he left Washington, it was obvious that John Tyler's political career had come to an end. He knew that he could never again be elected president, even if all his children were eligible to vote.

HIGHLIGHTS OF THE ADMINISTRATION OF JOHN TYLER

- 1841—Tyler's entire cabinet resigns after he vetoes banking bills supported by his Whig Party.

- 1844—Tyler signs Treaty of China, which opens trade to the Far East.

- 1845—Texas is annexed to the United States following the war with Mexico.

JAMES KNOX POLK (1795–1849)

State Born: North Carolina   Occupation: Lawyer

Party: Democrat   Religion: Methodist

JAMES KNOX
POLK

ELEVENTH PRESIDENT

1845–1849

Mrs. Polk being a member of the Presbyterian Church, I usually attend that church with her, though my opinions and predilections are in favor of the Methodist Church.

—JAMES KNOX POLK

His middle name, identical to the pioneer of the Presbyterian Church in Scotland, was no accident, for Jane Knox, the mother of President James Knox Polk, was a direct descendant of the famous John Knox. As we might expect, the president's upbringing included daily Bible readings, prayers, and a solid indoctrination in Calvinistic traditions.

FAMILY DISTRUST OF PRESBYTERIANS

The Reverend James Wallis, a local Presbyterian minister, demanded that the boy's parents both give a verbal confession of faith before the service of baptism. Samuel Polk stubbornly refused to take such an oath, so young James was never baptized into the Presbyterian fellowship.

One other fact entered the picture. All six children by the second marriage of his grandfather, Ezekiel Polk, were stillborn. Since the Presbyterian dogma of that era included the belief that the souls of unbaptized infants were damned to eternal death, most of the Polk family would have nothing to do with Presbyterianism.

The animosity between Sam Polk and Reverend Wallis grew so intense that the family left their home in North Carolina and moved to the friendlier territory of Tennessee.

Marriage to a Powerful Woman

Ironically, in 1824, James Knox Polk married Sarah Childress, a devout Presbyterian. Sarah had tremendous influence on her husband even after Polk was elected president. At the inaugural ball on March 4, 1845, for example, because of the First Lady's strong Presbyterian stance, all dancing and service of cocktails were halted for the two hours that the Polks were in attendance. This caused Sam Houston of Texas to say that the only thing wrong with President Polk was that he "drank too much water."

But President Polk stood by these convictions. His wife's Calvinistic heritage, for instance, permitted no work on Sunday, so President Polk made certain that this applied to the White House as well. Once, when the French minister visited the Executive Mansion on a Sunday, he was greeted by a servant who politely told the minister that the president never received guests on the Christian Sabbath.

During his term in office, President Polk accompanied Sarah to church regularly, but his personal loyalties were with another communion. He wrote in his diary for November 2, 1845, "Mrs.

Polk being a member of the Presbyterian Church, I usually attend that church with her, though my opinions and predilections are in favor of the Methodist Church."

According to the president, his preference for the Methodist Church was the direct result of the preaching of the Reverend John B. McFerrin. When Mr. Polk was thirty-eight years old, he was deeply affected by the minister's call to a self-awakening. Polk and McFerrin soon became lifelong friends.

A One-Term President

Part of the self-awakening for John Knox Polk may have been the realization that he no longer wished to be president of the United States. He, therefore, was the first president not to seek reelection.

Four months after leaving the Executive Mansion and less than a week before his death, Polk severed all religious ties with the Presbyterians. He volunteered to be baptized and was received into the Methodist fellowship by none other than his friend, the Reverend John B. McFerrin.

HIGHLIGHTS OF THE ADMINISTRATION OF JAMES KNOX POLK

- 1845—Florida and Texas become states.

- 1846—United States and Britain settle the dispute over Oregon Territory, accepting the 49th parallel as the fixed United States-Canadian boundary.

- 1846—Iowa becomes a state.

- 1848—Treaty of Guadalupe Hidalgo gives United States control over California, New Mexico, Arizona, Nevada, Utah, plus parts of Wyoming and Colorado. Mexico recognizes the Rio Grande as the southern boundary of Texas.

- 1848—Wisconsin becomes a state.

ZACHARY TAYLOR (1784–1850)

State Born: Virginia   Occupation: Soldier

Party: Whig   Religion: Unaffiliated (attended
Episcopal)

ZACHARY
TAYLOR

TWELFTH PRESIDENT
1849–1850

The idea that I should become president seems to me too visionary to require a
serious answer. It has never entered my head, nor is it likely to enter the head
of any sane person.

—ZACHARY TAYLOR

When the stocky-built, five-foot-eight-inch, one-hundred-seventy-pounder was an army lieutenant, Zachary Taylor was a tobacco-chewing, hard-cussing soul who earned the nickname "Old Rough and Ready." Ready for the White House? Hardly, for he never considered himself as "presidential timber." Ready for the church? Definitely not.

SILENCE ABOUT HIS FAITH

Regarded by most as an Episcopalian, Zachary Taylor joined no church, nor, as far as we know, made any public confession of religious belief.

In sharp contrast, his wife, Margaret, was a solid Episcopalian who, while with her husband at various military stations during his army career, organized worship services for those unable to attend a regular house of worship in town.

Although President Zachary Taylor occasionally worshiped at St. John's Episcopal Church, his appearances may have been solely out of his respect for his wife, who was then a semi-invalid and confined her public appearances to attendance at church.

The only hint we have as to any religious conviction on his part comes from his youngest daughter, Betty Taylor Bliss, who said of her father, "He was a constant reader of the Bible and practiced all its precepts, acknowledging his responsibility to God."

A FALLEN HERO

At his unexpected death rumored to be from pneumonia—due to overexposure on a muggy Fourth of July ceremony at the laying of the cornerstone for the Washington Monument in 1850—Zachary Taylor served as president for a term of only 492 days. The public was saddened at the loss of a rugged folk hero.

Praises about military victories and bold leadership echoed from city halls throughout the nation about the fallen president. Few contemporaries, however, found much to say about his accomplishments or, as a matter of fact, about his religious convictions.

HIGHLIGHTS OF THE ADMINISTRATION OF ZACHARY TAYLOR

- 1849—California Gold Rush
- 1850—Clayton-Bulwer Treaty guarantees that future canals crossing Central America will be available to all nations.

MILLARD FILLMORE (1800–1874)

State Born: New York   Occupation: Teacher/Lawyer

Party: Whig   Religion: Unitarian

MILLARD FILLMORE

THIRTEENTH PRESIDENT

1850–1853

Where is the true-hearted American whose cheek does not tingle with shame to see our highest and most courted foreign missions filled by men of foreign birth to the exclusion of the native-born?

—MILLARD FILLMORE, 1856

In 1968, shortly after he was elected as acting president of Michigan State University, Dr. Walter Adams employed his wry wit and predicted that his role as the university's thirteenth president would parallel that of the nation's thirteenth president, Millard Fillmore. It was Dr. Adams's subtle way of hinting that his term and contributions at M.S.U. quite possibly would be forgotten as quickly as those of President Fillmore.

Outside of being remembered as the second vice president to ascend to the office of president due to the death of his predecessor, Millard Fillmore is recalled as the one who, years later, escorted President Abraham Lincoln to Sunday worship services at the Unitarian Church in Buffalo, New York.

An Anti-Catholic Feeling

When Fillmore expressed his religious convictions, he spoke more of what he was *against* than what he was *for*. For instance, he was a member of the Know-Nothing party, which called for the removal of all Roman Catholics from public office, lest the policies of a state or of the nation be dictated by the Vatican in Rome. After losing the election for governor of New York in 1844, Fillmore blamed his defeat on "abolitionists and foreign Catholics."

Raised in a Methodist environment in Locke, New York, by a father who owned just two books—a Bible and a hymnbook—Millard Fillmore never found it necessary to express his religious convictions in public. Instead, he enjoyed the more quiet contentment offered through the intellectual stance encouraged by the Unitarians.

The president's identification with the Unitarians was short-lived during his brief stay at the White House. After supporting legislation that abolished slave trade in Washington, D.C., Fillmore lent his support to the Fugitive Slave Act, which provided for the return of runaway slaves to their owners in the South. As a result of this one decision, the president lost not only his party's nomination for election in 1852, but also his standing in the Unitarian Society, which severely criticized him.

Deeply hurt by this rejection, Millard Fillmore left the fellowship and occasionally attended Baptist and Episcopal churches thereafter.

At his funeral in March 1874, a Baptist, an Episcopalian, and a Presbyterian presided. There was no Unitarian.

HIGHLIGHTS OF THE ADMINISTRATION OF MILLARD FILLMORE

- 1850—The Compromise of 1850 is signed.
- 1850—California becomes a state.

FRANKLIN PIERCE (1804–1869)

State Born: New Hampshire   Occupation: Lawyer/Public Official

Party: Democrat   Religion: Episcopal

FRANKLIN
PIERCE

FOURTEENTH PRESIDENT
1853–1857

Frank, I pity you—indeed I do, from the bottom of my heart.

—NATHANIEL HAWTHORNE
to Franklin Pierce,
commenting on Pierce's excessive drinking habit

The poet Robert Browning penned these immortal words:

God's in His heaven—
All's right with world!

Perhaps that's true, but only for those who feel they are on good terms with the Almighty. Franklin Pierce had a difficult time believing that he and his Lord were on speaking terms.

Raised in what might be called a classical Puritan tradition, Pierce struggled to reach the level of faithfulness he thought was demanded by the Lord. At Bowdoin College, where he became a close friend with classmate Nathaniel Hawthorne, his guilt increased. Any temptation on his part to relax and enjoy himself was not in line with the strict rules of his faith or his college: no drinking or eating in taverns, no attending the theater, no playing cards and gambling, and no loud and disorderly singing. In fact, any student at Bowdoin guilty of "profaning the Sabbath by amusement" was subject to suspension.

Struggle with Puritan Standards

Franklin Pierce was never able to shake this yoke of Puritan standards even after he was elected as our fourteenth president. For instance, during his swearing-in ceremony, he chose to "affirm" rather than "swear" to uphold the Constitution and to defend the United States. He also maintained the prevailing notion that any personal tragedy was God's punishment for specific sins. Consequently, the deaths of his three sons—the last, eleven-year-old Benjamin just eight weeks before his inauguration—weighed heavily upon his soul. It caused him to write to his law partner: "I have dwelt upon the truths of Divine revelation and have struggled to think and act in conformity with the precepts and commands of the New Testament—but with indifferent success as every man must who is not a humble and devoted Christian, to which character I can, I regret to say, make no pretension."

Pierce's wife, Jane, associated Benjamin's death in a train wreck with her husband's election to the presidency. Somehow she felt that their personal tragedy was God's punishment upon the family for seeking fame through a quest for the Oval Office.

The First Lady's Depression

Jane Pierce was so affected by this tragedy that she refused to attend her husband's inauguration on January 6, 1853, when the new president said toward the end of his lengthy, memorized address: "There is no national security but in the nation's humble, acknowledged dependence upon God and His overruling providence." Jane Pierce could not accept this. If God was so cruel to her and her husband, how could he look with favor upon the nation?

During his four years in office, the president and his wife occasionally attended both Presbyterian churches in the nation's capital, steadfastly observed a "laborless Sabbath," and took turns leading the family prayers. However, none of these acts of devotion were enough to comfort Jane Pierce. She remained conspicuously absent from the whirlwind of Washington politics and society, seldom attending the social events normally demanding the presence of the nation's First Lady.

Her shyness developed into a deep melancholy over Benjamin's untimely death. She was so distraught that she wore black dresses every day of the week and spent much of her time sitting alone in her bedroom, writing notes to "Bennie," as she affectionately called him.

THE PRESIDENT'S BATTLE WITH ALCOHOL

Despite his Puritan heritage, Pierce assuaged his grief by frequent capitulation to his love for alcohol, each indulgence resulting in another dose of guilt. That guilt led to more and more consumption. It wasn't just a trained psychologist who could realize that the president developed a pattern with a hopeless spiral. Some of his political enemies declared that the president was "the hero of many a well-fought *bottle.*"

After his wife's death in 1863, Pierce gave up his fight against liquor. He simply resigned himself to the conviction that he would never win in his battle for sobriety.

Two years later, he was baptized in St. Paul's Episcopal Church, Concord, New Hampshire. It was a church that did not stress abstinence from alcohol as did the Presbyterians of that era. It was also a house of worship that he could attend, said Pierce, "without hearing a sermon on politics."

For Franklin Pierce, this may have been the only time he was "right with the world."

HIGHLIGHTS OF THE ADMINISTRATION OF FRANKLIN PIERCE

- 1853—Gadsen Purchase sets border with Mexico and gives the United States the land that is now New Mexico and Arizona for $10 million.

- 1854—Kansas-Nebraska Act establishes the territories of Nebraska and Kansas.

- 1854—Ostend Manifesto, a secret document, demands that Spain sell Cuba to the United States. The U.S. later disclaimed any official endorsement.

- 1854—Treaty with Japan opens trade with the United States.

JAMES BUCHANAN (1791–1868)

State Born: Pennsylvania

Occupation: Lawyer

Party: Democrat

Religion: Presbyterian

JAMES BUCHANAN

FIFTEENTH PRESIDENT
1857–1861

There are portions of the Union in which if you emancipate your slaves they will become your masters. Is there any man who would for a moment, indulge the horrible idea of abolishing slavery by the massacre of the chivalrous race of men in the South?

—James Buchanan

I have never known any human being for whom I felt a greater reverence," wrote James Buchanan of Dr. John King, a Presbyterian minister of his family's small church in Mercersburg, Pennsylvania, who also served on the board of nearby Dickinson College in Carlisle. Undoubtedly, Buchanan's accolade was promoted by Dr. King's influence to have young James reinstated at Dickinson after the spirited student was expelled for arrogance, disorderly conduct, and drinking.

James Buchanan

A Love Affair Turned Sour

Several years later, even Dr. King was unable to comfort his former student when young James was rejected by his fiancée, Ann Caroline Coleman, in part because of her father's suspicion that James was interested only in her money. (Mr. Coleman was a wealthy manufacturer; James, who was born in a log cabin, came from poor stock.) In addition, local gossips circulated unconfirmed rumors about Buchanan and another girl. During the next few months, Ann slipped deeper and deeper into a mental depression and later became mysteriously ill. She died from what physicians called "hysterical convulsions." Embittered members of her family, led by Mr. Coleman, branded Buchanan her murderer.

An Unforgiving Father

Overcome by grief, Buchanan wrote a letter to Ann's father requesting permission to view the body and join the mourners at her funeral. "It is now no time for explanation, but the time will come when you will discover that she, as well as I, have been much abused. God forgive the authors of it. I may sustain the shock of her death, but I feel that happiness has fled from me forever." The letter was returned to Buchanan unopened, and he was not allowed to attend the funeral.

Punishment from God

Close friends of the twenty-eight-year-old lawyer reported that he felt the pangs of guilt for many years thereafter and was convinced that God was certainly punishing him for past transgressions (a strong Calvinistic teaching in those days). Although he enjoyed the company of young ladies, Buchanan never married, making him our only bachelor president.

After his election to the presidency, Mr. Buchanan had other struggles with his personal faith. Because he was raised in an environment that equated Christianity with a Puritan lifestyle, the president realized that he was unable to rid himself of the belief that an Almighty God was punishing him for his inability or unwillingness to overcome temptations of this world. In his mounting frustration, he wrote to his minister brother, "I desire, so much, to be a Christian," sounding like the man who begged Jesus to heal his son in Mark 9:24: "Lord, I believe; help my unbelief." If we wish to label President Buchanan's religious conviction, it would be to say he was a "seeker."

In August 1860, Mr. Buchanan had a long, heart-to-heart conversation with the Reverend William Paxton, pastor of New York City's First Presbyterian Church. At the end of this meeting, the president announced, "My mind is made up. I hope that I am a Christian. As soon as I retire from office as president, I will unite with the Presbyterian Church." He felt that uniting with a congregation while in office might be construed by his opponents as a political move. He figured he would avoid all this simply by joining a church after leaving the Oval Office.

A Stumbling Block to Church Membership

It didn't turn out to be quite that easy. Buchanan had endorsed slavery on a limited scale and had spoken out sharply against emancipation while president. He was refused in his first attempt to gain membership in the northern Presbyterian Church, which advocated abolition. It wasn't until September 23, 1865, nearly four years after he left office, that Buchanan was permitted to make public profession of his faith and was invited to join the fellowship in "the church of my fathers," as he himself described it. In his last will and testament, Buchanan left a sizeable contribution to the Presbyterian Church.

On the afternoon before he died on June 1, 1868, as he lay ill in his mansion, Wheatland, near Lancaster, Pennsylvania, the former president said, "Whatever the result may be, I shall carry to my grave the consciousness that I at least meant well for my country."

That would have made Dr. King very happy indeed.

HIGHLIGHTS OF THE ADMINISTRATION OF JAMES BUCHANAN

- 1858—Minnesota becomes a state.
- 1859—Oregon becomes a state.
- 1860—Democrat Party splits into Northern and Southern wings over the issues of states' rights and slavery.
- 1861—Kansas becomes a state.

ABRAHAM LINCOLN (1809–1865)

State Born: Kentucky

Occupation: Lawyer

Party: Republican

Religion: Unaffiliated

ABRAHAM LINCOLN

SIXTEENTH PRESIDENT

1861–1865

If ever there lived a president who, during his term of service, needed all the consolation and the strength that he could draw from the Unseen Power above him, it was President Lincoln—sad, patient, mighty Lincoln, who worked and suffered for the people. . . . If there ever was a man who practically applied what was taught in our churches, it was Abraham Lincoln.

—Theodore Roosevelt, 1903

He was all things to all men. To the slave, he was the Messiah; to the press, he was the Rail-splitter; to the North, he was the Preserver of the Union; to the South that knew the Civil War was about to end, he was the Compassionate Victor.

To the Christian, he could well have been Champion of the Faith, except for one thing. Abraham Lincoln never joined a church.

"Nonsense," some say. "President Lincoln was one of our most God-fearing Americans."

But look at the record: Lincoln never joined a Christian congregation. Consequently a few scholars are bold enough to ask, "Was Abraham Lincoln a Christian?"

EARLY ACCUSATIONS

Their question is not new. It was raised even when Honest Abe began his political career in New Salem, Illinois—where he arrived in 1831, as he said, like "a piece of floating driftwood." During his six years there he became friends with Jack Kelso, the village philosopher, who introduced the young Lincoln to the writings of Shakespeare and the teachings of the Bible. Lincoln studied them earnestly, even memorizing long passages. His speeches and private letters often echo the seventeenth-century tone of Shakespeare or the King James Version of the Bible.

In spite of his familiarity with and love of the Bible, Lincoln still never became a member of a local Christian church. And his early political opponents used this as an opportunity to brand him an infidel.

LINCOLN'S DEFENSE ON THE CAMPAIGN TRAIL

Lincoln defended his decision: "I doubt the possibility or propriety of settling the religion of Jesus Christ in the models of man-made creeds and dogmas. I cannot without mental reservations assent to long and complicated creeds and catechisms."

His answer fell on deaf ears. Meanwhile Lincoln earned a reputation in that tiny community as an outspoken nonbeliever. He certainly didn't help his cause when he openly discussed the writings of Thomas Paine, an avowed agnostic, and enjoyed arguing in private with friends against some church practices.

Because of the sensitivity of his neighbors about the subject, Lincoln avoided the issue whenever possible. "Religion," he said on many occasions, "is a private affair between a man and his God." Later, during his 1846 congressional campaign, he was compelled to meet the issue head-on. His opponent—Peter Cartwright, a well-known Methodist circuit rider—openly charged that Lincoln was an atheist and an enemy of the organized church.

"That I am not a member of any Christian church is true," Lincoln confessed, "but I have never denied the truth of the Scriptures, and I have never spoken with intentional disrespect of religion in general or of any denomination of Christians in particular."

Lincoln won the election by a landslide, even though his answer didn't satisfy everyone, especially the local clergy.

LINCOLN'S FIRST INAUGURAL

Abraham Lincoln's most important political victory came fifteen years later when he climbed the steps of the U.S. Capitol, placed his left hand on a Bible, and swore to "faithfully execute the office of president of the United States." He entered the White House with the challenge to direct the course of a nation not yet a century old that was about to war with itself.

The poet Goethe may have had someone like Lincoln in mind when he wrote, "God contrives to send during critical moments in history great genius to solve great problems." Part of Lincoln's genius is reflected in his willingness to shun certain things—including an endorsement of one denomination over another—that might further divide the country.

Knowing Lincoln's religious character, one member of Congress asked him why he never joined a church. Lincoln replied, "Because I have found difficulty, without mental reservation, in giving my assent to their long and complicated confessions of faith. When any church will inscribe over its altar the Savior's condensed statement of law and gospel: 'Thou shalt love the Lord thy God with all thy heart and with all thy soul and with all thy mind, and love thy neighbor as thyself,' that church will I join with all my heart."

Although he remained unwilling to sign his name on the

membership rolls of a particular congregation, Lincoln showed respect for the organized church during some of the more important stages of his career. For instance, he recited his marriage vows to Mary Todd on November 4, 1842, before the Reverend Charles Dresser, an Episcopal priest, and he chose to attend a special service of worship conducted at St. John's Episcopal Church in Washington on the day before his first inauguration.

LINCOLN'S UNIQUE APPROACH TO THE CHURCH

Lincoln's refusal to join an organized church still gave rise to many doubts about his belief in God. Lincoln himself enjoyed repeating an often-told story about two Quaker women who discussed his potential success as compared to that of Jefferson David, president of the Confederate States:

"I think Jefferson will succeed," said one woman.

"Why does thee think so?" asked the other.

"Because Jefferson is a praying man."

"And so is Abraham a praying man."

"Yes, but the Lord will think Abraham is joking."

In spite of the gossip and jokes floating around Washington, Lincoln showed a personal attachment to the Presbyterian Church. He rented a pew, a custom of that era, in Washington's New York Avenue Presbyterian Church (located on the right side of the church, eight rows from the pulpit). He and his family regularly worshiped there on Sunday mornings.

On several occasions the president even attended midweek prayer meetings at this church. But in order not to disturb other worshipers, Lincoln often secretly entered through the back door of the building, sat on a settee in the office of the pastor, Dr. Phineas Gurley, and, with the door to the church ajar, listened to the readings from the Scriptures and prayed with the people.

One Sunday morning when Confederate forces drew close to the city and the fighting was heavy, Dr. Gurley declared from his pulpit that the next Sunday would be the last in which the church could be used for worship. An order from Secretary of War Stanton had requisitioned the church for use as a hospital for wounded soldiers.

President Lincoln, who was attending worship that day, rose to his feet and said, "Dr. Gurley, we are too much in need of this church these days; we cannot let it be closed. I countermand the order."

Lincoln publicly spoke about this dependence upon help from Almighty God not only in church but on other occasions as well. In February 1861, for example, as he was about to leave for Washington to begin his first term as president, he stood on the rear platform of the Great Western Railway train and spoke heart to heart with his close friends and neighbors of Springfield, Illinois:

> I now leave not knowing when, or whether ever, I may return, with a task before me greater than that which rested upon [George] Washington. Without the assistance of that Divine Being who ever attended him I cannot succeed. With that assistance, I cannot fail. Trusting in him, let us confidently hope that all will yet be well. To his care commending you, I hope in your prayers you will commend me. I bid you an affectionate farewell.

Lincoln also spoke of his dependence upon the guiding hand of God and his faith in the promises of the Bible, especially during moments of anxiety.

Less than a year following the death of his four-year-old son, Eddie, Lincoln learned of his father's serious illness from his stepbrother John Johnston. Lincoln's letter to his stepbrother reveals the clearest expression we have of his concept of immortality:

> Tell father to remember to call upon and confide in our great, and good, and merciful Maker who will not turn away from him in any extremity. He notes the fall of a sparrow and numbers the hairs of

our heads; and he will not forget the dying man who puts his trust in him. If it is to be his lot to go now, he will soon have a joyous meeting with many loved ones gone before; and where the rest of us, through the help of God, hope ere long to join them.

On the morning of the funeral of another son—eleven-year-old Willie in 1862—a shaken President Lincoln was comforted by the boy's nurse, who assured him that Christians throughout the nation were praying for him.

"I am glad to hear that," replied the president. "I need their prayers. I will try to go to God with my sorrows."

THE CIVIL WAR

The horrors of the Civil War during the troubled years that followed gnawed at him. Abraham Lincoln nonetheless kept his courage through private prayer.

A fact well documented in the records of the New York Avenue Presbyterian Church is that before an important battle or at the news of some crisis, whether day or night, the president sent his carriage to bring Pastor Gurley to the White House. There, the two of them spent hours praying for the Lord's guidance.

Lincoln later commented, "I have been driven many times to my knees in prayer by the overwhelming conviction that I had nowhere else to go. My wisdom and all that about me seemed insufficient for the day."

To a delegation from the Baltimore Presbyterian Synod he repeated this admission; "Amid the greatest difficulties of my administration, when I could not see any other resort, I would place my whole reliance on God."

Illinois Senator Lyman Trumbull once complimented the president on his ever-present optimism during the hectic days of the war.

"Mr. President," he said, "on Capitol Hill we all wonder that you can do so well in these trying times, especially as you have no precedent to guide you in anything, judicial, civil or military."

"Please tell the boys on Capitol Hill that I have precedents for everything," replied the president. "Tell them all that I shall commit no dangerous error; that I shall not blunder, because I have precedents, and I carefully follow them. I get my precedents by my bedside at night. I get them while I am on my knees. I seek my precedents then and there; and they come to me from the source of all wisdom."

Kneeling in private prayer was not uncommon for Abraham Lincoln, but his posture was strikingly different at public worship. Normally, Presbyterians of that day sat in their pews for prayer during services. Lincoln, however, stood while praying. His angular, ungainly six-foot-four-inch frame created an awkward contrast while those around him sat with bowed heads.

After one worship service, a curious parishioner got enough courage to ask him about his unusual posture during prayer. Lincoln explained, "When my generals visit the White House, they stand when their commander in chief enters the Oval Office. Isn't it proper, then, that I stand for *my* commander in chief?"

Lincoln's pragmatic theology helped keep things in perspective. There was the time one devout Christian expressed hope that "the Lord would be on our side." The president responded, "I am not concerned about that, for I know that the Lord is *always* on the side of the *right*. But it is my constant anxiety and prayer that I and the nation should be on the *Lord's* side."

In fact, religion for Abraham Lincoln was always a practical application of biblical truths as the situation called for them. He could be stern when scolding people who shirked their responsibility to earn their daily bread "by the sweat of their brows"; he could be benevolent when he commuted the death sentence of a young soldier who fell asleep while on guard duty. In an era when conservative Christians condemned anyone who attended the theater—"a den of painted women and rogues," they said—Lincoln enjoyed watching plays as a means of escape from pressures of the White House.

LINCOLN AND SLAVERY

Some historians suggest that Lincoln's freeing the slaves was the result of some deep religious or moral conviction. We have no evidence to prove such a claim. Instead, his primary concern was the preservation of the Union. He repeated often that if maintaining the practice of slavery would guarantee the unity of the nation, he would endorse it; but he would also free the slaves if that would save the Union.

He hinted at a moral justification in an 1862 message to Congress when he said, "In giving freedom to the slave we assure freedom to the free. . . . The way is plain, peaceful, generous, just—a way, if followed, the world will forever applaud, and God must forever bless."

On January 1, 1863, when he issued the Emancipation Proclamation, Lincoln added, "Upon this act, sincerely believed to be an act of justice, warranted by the Constitution . . . I invoke the considerate judgment of mankind and the gracious favor of Almighty God."

A SÉANCE IN THE WHITE HOUSE

President Lincoln said other things that would please even the most orthodox theologian. On the other hand, he was not above what he called "experimenting" with religion.

In April 1863, probably in order to please his wife, who was interested in such things since the loss of their son Willie, Lincoln hosted a spiritual seance in the Red Room of the White House. The medium claimed to reveal secrets "from beyond" through eerie voices that seemed to come from above them. Lincoln treated the whole business lightly, observing that the strange language "sounded very much like the babbling of my cabinet."

Abraham Lincoln is the most quoted of all the American presidents. We are fortunate to have copies of his major speeches and many of his personal letters. Together they paint a portrait of a man who must be labeled one of America's greatest theologians. Certainly not in the classical sense of the word—he neither drafted a system of biblical doctrine nor defended a particular denomination. Yet he was quick to recognize the hand of Almighty God working in the affairs of nations.

In this regard he sounded like the prophets of the Old Testament who interpreted events of their day through the eyes of God. Lincoln became a latter-day prophet who saw God as the author of history.

"If the truth must be known, Abraham Lincoln was a fatalist," said his former law partner, William Herndon. Quoting Shakespeare, Lincoln's friend Henry Whitney agreed, "He believed and often said, 'There's a divinity that shapes our ends, rough-hew them how we will.'"

A Vision in the East Room

One morning shortly before his death, Lincoln shared with his friend Ward Lamon and his wife a dream he had the night before in which he heard invisible mourners in the White House. He walked into the East Room where he saw a catafalque with a corpse guarded by soldiers.

"Who's dead in the White House?" he demanded of one.

"The president," came the reply. "He was killed by an assassin."

Lincoln turned to Lamon and Mary and added, "It seems strange how much there is in the Bible about dreams. There are, I think, some sixteen chapters in the Old Testament and four or five in the New in which dreams are mentioned. If we believe the Bible we must accept the fact that in the old days God and his angels came to men in their sleep and made themselves known in dreams."

Lincoln may well have been a fatalist, but not in the sense that he believed that God did whatever he wanted so all people, both good and evil, suffered the same consequences. Lincoln felt that God's favors were there for those who asked for them.

For example, Lincoln set aside April 30, 1863, as a national day of humiliation and fasting. In his official pronouncement he wrote, "It is the duty of nations, as well of men, to confess their sins and transgressions. . . . yet with assured hope that genuine repentance will lead to mercy and pardon, and to recognize the sublime truth announced in the Holy Scriptures and proven by all history that those nations only are blessed whose God is the Lord."

Later that same year, following major victories of the Union army at Vicksburg and other strategic cities, Lincoln revealed more of his personal theology: "No human counsel hath devised nor hath any mortal hand worked out these great things. They are the gracious gifts of the Most High God who, while dealing with us in anger for our sins, hath nevertheless remembered mercy."

On November 19, 1863, he quite probably repeated that theme in his famous Gettysburg Address "that this nation, under God, shall have a new birth of freedom."

Scholars today continue to debate whether or not Lincoln used the phrase "under God" in his speech; these words did not appear in the first draft. Lincoln did, however, include them in future hand-written copies of the text.

Lincoln firmly believed that the hand of God would determine the outcome of the Civil War. "The substantial dispute," he said, was between the section that "believes slavery is right and ought to be extended, and the other that believes it is wrong and ought not to be extended." He then added that God's verdict would sooner or later be made evident by "the judgment of this great tribunal, the American people."

LEGENDS STILL ABOUND

Lincoln's creed, like other dimensions of his life, was simple and practical. It was based on the teachings of the Bible, coupled with our obligation to seek the help of God. Yet this childlike faith has been butchered by those who attempted to turn the man into something he was not. Consequently, Americans have been robbed of the opportunity to know the rich human side of this man who shaped the future of the Union.

For instance, a few days following the president's assassination, on April 14, 1865, by John Wilkes Booth at Ford's Theatre in Washington, two respected clergymen of Springfield testified that Lincoln had made a special trip from Washington, where he was baptized at night in the flowing waters of a river. White House records and the president's diary fail to substantiate these claims.

A Roman Catholic priest claimed Lincoln received the sacrament of baptism secretly. No records support this claim either.

Another story from a member of the New York Avenue Presbyterian Church quotes Pastor Gurley as saying that Lincoln had every intention of formally joining the congregation on the Easter Sunday following the end of the Civil War. Again, official records do not confirm this.

Even if this last story were true, we'll never know. As that Easter Sunday dawned, Americans were still weeping for their fallen leader who, on Good Friday, had attended Ford's Theater and was torn from the nation by an assassin's bullet.

Was Abraham Lincoln a Christian? For those convinced that

Christianity equates itself solely with church membership, the book is closed. For others, the way he demonstrated his faith in the Lord was more than enough evidence to say yes.

Yet there still remain unanswered questions about his faith that enhance the mystery surrounding him—a mystery that can be solved only by Lincoln's own "commander in chief."

HIGHLIGHTS OF THE ADMINISTRATION OF ABRAHAM LINCOLN

- 1861—Civil War begins.
- 1863—West Virginia becomes a state.
- 1863—The Emancipation Proclamation gives freedom to slaves.
- 1863—Lincoln delivers the Gettysburg Address.
- 1864—"In God We Trust" is added to U.S. coins.
- 1864—Nevada becomes a state.
- 1864—Lincoln is reelected to a second term.
- 1865—Civil War ends.
- 1865—Lincoln becomes the first president to be assassinated.

ANDREW JOHNSON (1808–1875)

State Born: North Carolina   Occupation: Tailor

Party: Democrat   Religion: Unaffiliated

ANDREW JOHNSON

SEVENTEENTH PRESIDENT
1865–1869

*Let us stand as equals in the Union, all upon equality. Let peace and union be
restored to the land. May God bless this people and
God save the Constitution.*

—ANDREW JOHNSON,
from his last Senate speech

Maybe it was his discovery that some Protestant clergymen actually asked public prayers for his conviction in his impeachment hearings in 1868 that discouraged Andrew Johnson from identifying with any particular Christian denomination while in Washington.

AN UPHILL FIGHT

The man who is best remembered as the man to succeed the slain Abraham Lincoln and as the first president to be impeached, faced an impossible situation. Living in the shadow of a giant like Lincoln, Johnson had extreme difficulty in convincing others that he was carrying out the Great Emancipator's reconstruction program for the battered South. When he declared, "Treason must be made infamous, and traitors must be punished," many linked him with the radicals. Although Johnson was referring only to military and political leaders of the Confederacy, he faced an uphill fight in gaining support.

He did other things to generate political enemies. After President Lincoln's death, some patriotic Northerners thought this poor white man—the only president who never set foot in a schoolroom—would lash out at the South and punish those who sought to split the Union. Their hopes were dashed when Johnson refused to embrace their philosophy. At the same time, when the nation was beginning to appreciate the ideals of Lincoln, President Johnson sounded an alarm about the potential danger of allowing blacks to vote. "Of all the dangers which our nation has yet encountered," he said, "none are equal to those which must result from success of the current effort to 'Africanize' the southern half of the country."

IMPEACHMENT

Eventually this one-man effort to suppress the rights of blacks, coupled with his refusal to join the ranks of those in Congress eager to humiliate the defeated South, led to his impeachment by the House of Representatives. Johnson's removal from office, requiring a two-thirds vote by the Senate, fell one vote short.

What few supporters Johnson gained through this move, he lost when he refused to endorse the Know Nothing party's attempts to restrict the liberties of the Roman Catholic Church. Johnson would not accept, as did some of his forerunners, the concept that "foreign Catholics" in influential government positions were a threat to America's security. To those who believed this, the president posed the rhetorical questions: "Who was John Wesley? Who was Martin

Luther? Were they alive today, would they be driven back to the countries from which they came?"

While his advocacy of suppression of blacks created enemies for President Johnson on one side of the political fence, his closeness with the Catholics was the real slap in the face for those who endorsed the presidential tradition.

Contributing to the lack of trust of Catholics was the rumor that the Roman Catholic Church was somehow involved in a conspiracy to assassinate President Lincoln. Several people, including the only woman hanged for the conspiracy to assassinate Lincoln—Mary Surratt—were Roman Catholics.

Adding fuel to the flames of gossip were accusations, including one from Mary Todd Lincoln that Johnson, himself, played a role in President Lincoln's assassination.

Favoring the Roman Catholic Church

President Johnson not only tolerated the Roman Catholic Church, he personally endorsed it with his presence at Sunday mass. On more than one occasion, he attended worship services at St. Patrick's Catehdral in Washington, D.C. where, as he said, he could count on Father McGuire "not to preach a sermon on politics." In addition, the president publicly praised the Roman Catholic Church for its willingness to treat both rich and poor alike.

It was obvious to his closest friends and advisers that Mr. Johnson's personal allegiance was to the Roman Catholic communion. Had circumstances and times been different, he probably would have converted to the Catholic faith. But two things stood in his way.

First, joining the Roman Catholic Church would have been political suicide. Second, his wife, Eliza, a dedicated Methodist who was an invalid for twenty years, would have been crushed had her husband made such a move. Consequently, although his wife was unable to attend church services, the president, for her sake, worshiped mostly at Washington's Methodist churches.

Deep in his heart, however, Andrew Johnson was a Roman Catholic. Perhaps this was the only church he could attend without fear of some clergyman praying against him.

Following his term in office, the former president sat in the front pew at the dedication of St. Patrick's Catholic Church in his hometown of Greeneville, Tennessee, and gave a generous gift of five hundred dollars to its building fund.

However, when Andrew Johnson died at his home in Tennessee in 1875, the Masonic lodge to which he belonged conducted his funeral.

HIGHLIGHTS OF THE ADMINISTRATION OF ANDREW JOHNSON

- 1865—The Thirteenth Amendment to the Constitution abolishes slavery.

- 1866—The Civil Rights Bill guarantees the basic civil rights of freedmen.

- 1867—Nebraska becomes a state.

- 1868—The Fourteenth Amendment extends citizenship to former slaves.

- 1868—The Fifteenth Amendment guarantees former slaves the right to vote.

- 1868—Johnson becomes the first president to be impeached.

ULYSSES SIMPSON GRANT (1822–1885)

State Born: Ohio

Party: Republican

Occupation: Soldier

Religion: Unaffiliated
(attended Methodist)

ULYSSES SIMPSON GRANT

EIGHTEENTH PRESIDENT

1869–1877

*Leave the matter of religion to the family altar, the church, and the private
school, supported entirely by private contributions.
Keep the church and the state forever separate.*

—ULYSSES S. GRANT

Frankly speaking, history has given him a raw deal.

Like some others who occupied the White House before and after him, Ulysses Simpson Grant is best remembered for heading an administration fraught with scandal. A widespread spoils system employed by successful political candidates resulted in the appointment of less-than-capable cronies to high government positions. Subsequent investigations uncovered a misuse of funds by Grant's secretary of the treasury and secretary of war, among others.

On top of this, the financial panic of September 1873, which forced several important eastern banks to close, gave plenty of ammunition to his enemies, who dumped the blame entirely upon

President Grant. But Grant stonewalled with the same spirit that caused his former commander in chief, Abraham Lincoln, to confess, "I cannot spare this man; he fights."

"I never forsake a friend," President Grant often said, although many times he probably should have. In standing by his friends, the president became the victim to guilt by association. Nonetheless, even his worst enemies had to admit that Grant was basically an honest individual who suffered from the not-so-honest dealings of those he selected to surround him. History books seldom if ever, mention this fact.

The same books picture this five-foot-eight-inch, red-bearded, stoop-shouldered president as a semi-intelligent (he graduated twenty-ninth in his class of thirty-nine at West Point), gruff, impersonal man without much compassion. But let's consider the facts.

A Pragmatic General

As supreme commander of the Union armies during America's Civil War, Ulysses S. Grant was unmerciful in soundly defeating the Confederate Army and its general, Robert E. Lee. "The art of war is simple enough," said Grant. "Find out where your enemy is. Get at him as soon as you can. Strike at him as hard as you can, and keep moving on."

Northerners proudly called him "Unconditional Surrender Grant." Yet after Lee's surrender at the Appomattox courthouse in 1865, Grant successfully fought with equal vigor for protection from punishment for Lee and his troops by the United States Congress. "The war is over," he said. "We've all had enough bloodshed."

He even made this philosophy a conspicuous point of his 1873 inaugural address, during which he made one of his infrequent references to Almighty God. "I do believe that our Great Maker is preparing the world, in his own good time, to become one nation . . . when armies and navies will be no longer required."

Any other acts of charity or hopes for universal peace expressed throughout the remainder of his life were in private. President Grant took little part in Washington's social activities and chose to remain a recluse, sheltered from outside alliances.

ABSENCE FROM ANY CHRISTIAN AFFILIATION

As far as the organized church was concerned, President Grant never affiliated with a specific Christian denomination, although he attended several Protestant churches with his wife, Julia. Most frequently the President and Mrs. Grant visited the Metropolitan Methodist Church (now the National Methodist Church), where early records list him, perhaps erroneously, as a trustee.

Perhaps the only relationship, if you call it that, Grant had with the church twofold. First, he said, "Leave the matter of religion to the family altar, the church, and the private school, supported entirely by private contributions. Keep the church and the state forever separate." Second, he was the only president who requested from Congress the taxation of church property.

On rare occasions, Grant did express a positive religious note. All his life, Grant had an aversion to any kind of profanity, and he allowed no off-color stories to be told in his presence. In an article he penned for the *Sunday School Times,* he advised the nation's children: "Hold fast to the Bible as the sheet anchor of your liberties; write its precepts in your hearts and practice them in your lives."

HIS USE OF ALCOHOL AND TOBACCO

The most publicized character flaw our history books claim about President Grant is that he was a drunkard. Grant himself encouraged stories about his alcohol problem with such statements as, "I have been convinced that there is no safety from ruin by liquor except by abstaining from it altogether."

While he did fight many battles with the bottle in his early career (once being forced to resign as a captain because of excessive drinking), Grant never became a slave to alcohol. By the time he reached the White House, he completely conquered any problem that he might have had in this regard. He even turned over his glass whenever the White House waiters served wine at the dinner table.

The president did, however, smoke twenty cigars a day, a habit disturbing to some fundamentalist Christians of his era, and one that undoubtedly contributed to the throat cancer that took his life when he was sixty-three years old.

In his autobiography titled *Memoirs,* that was quickly edited and published by Mark Twain, the general was forthright about his use of alcohol and tobacco throughout his life and career. In the same volume, he avoided any mention of his association with a church. In fact all the reliable records we have of the general would indicate that he had never expressed a belief in the divinity of Christ or endorsed any of the creeds of the Christian Church.

A PLOY TO "METHODIZE"

During the last three months of his life, Grant grew increasingly ill. He knew he was dying. Even during this critical time, the former president made no effort to make himself "right with God."

A story still making its rounds describes how, when he lay on his deathbed, he was subjected to a weak attempt to "Methodize" him. It occurred on the morning of July 23, 1885, when Mrs. Grant sent for the Reverend Dr. J. P. Newman to pray at her husband's side. As the former president was sinking into a coma, Newman sprinkled water on his brow and uttered the words of the service of baptism, after which he immediately announced that Grant had been "converted and baptized into the Methodist faith." When Grant regained some of his senses and was told what happened, he responded to the clergyman, "Tsk, tsk, you surprise me."

That's the sort of story by which President Grant would have liked to be remembered. Unfortunately, he didn't write the history books.

HIGHLIGHTS OF THE ADMINISTRATION OF ULYSSES SIMPSON GRANT

- 1869—Thomas Edison invents the voting machine.

- 1869—First transcontinental railroad is completed.

- 1876—Colorado becomes a state.

- 1876—Alexander Graham Bell invents the telephone.

- 1876—Battle of Little Big Horn is fought.

RUTHERFORD BIRCHARD HAYES (1822–1893)

State Born: Ohio   Occupation: Lawyer

Party: Republican   Religion: Unaffiliated

RUTHERFORD BIRCHARD HAYES

NINETEENTH PRESIDENT

1877–1881

I am a Christian according to my conscience, in belief, not, of course, in character and conduct, but in purpose and wish; not, of course, by orthodox standards. But I am content and have a feeling of trust and safety . . . Let me be pure and wise and kind and true in all things.

—RUTHERFORD B. HAYES,
from his diary entry, 1893, shortly before his death

I am a Christian," wrote Rutherford Birchard Hayes, thus making him one of the first men to occupy the White House who, without apparent reservation, publicly pronounced his religious convictions. At the same time, although he and his wife, Lucy, attended the Foundry Methodist Church in Washington, the president never became a member. In his diary, he wrote his justification: "I belong to no church. But . . . I try to be a Christian, or rather I want to help to do Christian work." Nevertheless, he did encourage his son, Webb, to attend and to join a church. "While the habit [churchgoing] does not Christianize," he told him, "it generally civilizes."

Later, President Hayes wrote in his diary, "What a great mistake the man makes who goes about to oppose this religion! What a crime, if we may judge of men's acts by their results! Nay, what a great mistake is made by him who does not support the religion of the Bible!"

"Lemonade Lucy"

Visitors to the White House, even today, are told by tour guides the story of how First Lady Lucy Hayes proved beneficial to her husband's career. She was an attractive, cultured lady who possessed a conservative Christian character. Her influence alone altered the style of Washington social life. She permitted no card playing, smoking, or dancing in the White House, and her unwavering antiliquor stance meant that no alcohol was served in the Executive Mansion. Her husband's enemies, as well as some friends, called her "Lemonade Lucy."

The Christian standards of the First Family did not end with mere personal prohibition. They displayed regular acts of devotion. Every morning, at breakfast, the president and Lucy held prayer readings, which ended with their kneeling and praying aloud the Lord's Prayer.

Sunday evening hymn sings were not uncommon either, with congressmen, cabinet members, and Vice President William A. Wheeler attending. Favorite hymns of President Hayes included "Jesus, Lover of My Soul," "Nearer, My God, to Thee," and "Blest Be the Tie That Binds."

A Disputed Start to the Office

In spite of all this, President Hayes did not enjoy the glories of the office. Part of the reason, of course, was due to the fact that in the election of 1876, Hayes was defeated by Samuel J. Tilden—the

Democratic Party's candidate—by more than 250,000 votes. An electoral commission determined, however, that disputed electoral votes in Florida, Oregon, Louisiana, and South Carolina should go to Hayes, thus giving him a 185 to 184 margin in electoral votes over Tilden in the Electoral College. Consequently, President Hayes announced that he would not seek a second term.

When his term ended in 1881, Rutherford Hayes confessed, "Nobody left the presidency with less regret, less disappointment, fewer heart-burnings, or any general content with the result of his term (in his own heart, I mean) than I do." After four years in the White House, he and Lucy happily traded the hustle and bustle of Washington for the peaceful tranquility of home and the opportunity to sit together, quietly, sharing a beautiful Ohio sunset . . . sipping lemonade.

HIGHLIGHTS OF THE ADMINISTRATION OF RUTHERFORD BIRCHARD HAYES

- 1877—Federal troops withdraw from the South.

- 1877—Thomas Edison invents the phonograph.

- 1878—Bland-Allison Act expands the opportunity to sell silver.

- 1879—President signs act allowing female attorneys to argue a case before the Supreme Court.

- 1879—Thomas Edison invents the incandescent light bulb.

JAMES ABRAM GARFIELD (1831–1881)

State Born: Ohio   Occupation: Teacher/Lawyer

Party: Republican   Religion: Disciples of Christ

JAMES ABRAM GARFIELD

TWENTIETH PRESIDENT

1881

Thanks be to God for His goodness. By the help of God,
I'll praise my Maker while I've breath.

—JAMES A. GARFIELD

It had to happen sooner or later. A preacher came to the White House.

James Abram Garfield, twentieth president of the United States, was a loyal member and sometimes lay preacher of the Disciples of Christ. "He transports a body to heaven with his very voice," said a listener to one of his sermons.

His messages to churches were akin to those of a traveling, tent-meeting evangelist. "I've come tonight to speak with this poor tongue about Jesus. I've come to ask you to do what I did when I was eighteen years old, to choose the undying Jesus as your friend and helper, because the hopes of the world are false and the Christian never dies."

103

CALLED FROM THE PULPIT TO POLITICS

After much soul-searching, the call to the political stage drew the young zealot away from the pulpit. The skills of rhetoric practiced in ecclesiastical circles proved a solid base for Garfield's ability to persuade in the political arena. For example, at the time of the assassination of President Abraham Lincoln in 1865, the newly elected Congressman Garfield soothed the anger of nearly ten thousand rioters in New York City by shouting, "Fellow citizens! God reigns, and the government at Washington still lives!"

DISCIPLES OF CHRIST

Even after his election as chief executive in 1880, this man who was born in a log cabin—the epitome of the rags-to-riches success story admired by most Americans—along with his wife Lucretia, maintained a deep devotion to the teachings of the Disciples of Christ. Garfield was therefore outspoken in his opposition to both war and slavery because he felt that they were contrary to the teachings of his church. The president echoed the basic teaching of the Disciples of Christ for his strong position: "Where the Bible is silent, there we are silent; where the Bible speaks, there we speak."

We can catch some of the fervent spirit of Garfield's faith when we read his personal testimony as recorded in his diary: "Thanks be to God for his goodness. By the help of God, I'll praise my Maker while I've breath."

ASSASSINATION

As it turns out, that wasn't to be for long. After only four months in office, on July 2, 1881, while waiting to board a train in Washington en route to attend the twenty-fifth reunion of his graduating class at Williams College in Williamstown, Massachusetts, President

Garfield was shot twice by Charles J. Guiteau. Guiteau was a mentally disturbed man who, according to biographer Glenn Kittler, believed that the president had turned into the embodiment of evil. Later, Guiteau claimed that he "tried to destroy the president wholly and solely for the good of the country and at the command of God."

For three months, Garfield lay suffering in excruciating pain. A shattered spine, a bullet in the pancreas hidden from the view of the physicians, and a condition too weak to risk surgery all took their toll.

On September 8, 1881, the president heard the pealing of church bells.

"Are they praying for me?" he asked Dr. Susan Edson, the attending physician.

"Yes," Dr. Edson replied, "the people of the entire country are praying for you."

"God bless them," said Garfield.

In less than two weeks, he whispered his last words: "I can hear it. I am prepared to die." Within a few hours, the preacher turned president joined a the church he sought all his life—the fellowship of the saints in heaven.

HIGHLIGHTS OF THE ADMINISTRATION OF JAMES ABRAM GARFIELD

- 1880—On election day, Garfield is the only person ever to be a member of the House, a senator-elect, and a president-elect all at the same time.

- 1880—Construction of the Panama Canal begins.

- 1880—Electric lights are installed on New York City streets.

- 1881—Garfield is shot.

CHESTER ALAN ARTHUR (1830–1886)

State Born: Vermont

Party: Republican

Occupation: Teacher/Lawyer

Religion: Unaffiliated
(attended Episcopal)

CHESTER ALAN ARTHUR

TWENTY-FIRST PRESIDENT
1881–1885

I assume the trust imposed on me by the Constitution,
relying for aid on Divine guidance and the
virtue, patriotism, and intelligence of the American people.

—CHESTER ALAN ARTHUR,
immediately following his taking
of the oath of office

Two Vermont towns lay claim to being his birthplace. Some historians even argue that he was born in Canada. These are but a few of the confusions and contradictions resulting from lack of an authorized biography of the man who served as the twenty-first president of the United States. Yet we do know enough to capture some of the personality—the lonely personality—of Chester Arthur.

His father, a rural Baptist minister in Fairfield, Vermont, schooled him in the basic teachings of the Christian faith. However, young Chester chose not to affiliate with the Baptist denomination or with any other branch of the church.

Love and Tragedy

The most influential person in Arthur's life, in terms of religious expressions, was the beautiful Ellen (Nell) Herndon, a devout Episcopalian, who sang in her church choir. When Arthur and Nell began their courtship, many of their first dates were trips together to Sunday morning worship services. After they were married, they continued to attend Episcopal services, although Arthur never identified with any specific congregation.

Perhaps, in time, Chester Arthur would have joined a church and become a staunch supporter of the faith. But even before he was elected vice president under James Garfield, his beloved Nell died. His friends reported that much of his zest for living seemed to die with her.

Death of President Garfield

On September 20, 1881, at one-thirty in the morning, in his home on Lexington Avenue in New York City, Chester Arthur was whisked into office at the sudden death of President Garfield. Two days later the still-shocked vice president again took an oath of office—this time for president—in the Capitol in Washington, D.C. There he placed his hand on a Bible opened to Psalm 21. He said that it reminded him of the *Te Deum* his wife used to sing in the choir when they attended church on Sunday mornings: "In Thee, O Lord, do I put my trust; let me never be ashamed. Deliver me in thy righteousness."

After the swearing-in ceremony, Arthur gave a brief, emotional statement that ended with a personal declaration: "I assume the trust imposed on me by the Constitution, relying for aid on Divine guidance and the virtue, patriotism, and intelligence of the American people."

A Lonely Presidency

The following years of presidency for Chester Arthur were lonely. One reporter wrote, "Surely no more lonely and pathetic figure was ever seen assuming the powers of government. He had no people behind him, for it was Garfield, not he, who was the people's choice. He was alone. He was bowed down by the weight of fearful responsibility."

Later, Arthur confessed, "Since I came here, I have learned that Chester A. Arthur is one man and the president of the United States is another."

As a widower, he was the subject of rumors about potential romances, and every available lady who attended a White House social function became the subject of another story. When the president ordered a fresh bouquet of flowers delivered to the White House each day, the gossip increased. But a persistent reporter discovered that the flowers were set before a portrait of the president's deceased wife, and the gossip ceased.

A man who was thrust into the presidency because of the death of his predecessor enters the Oval Office with limited credibility. Couple this with some malicious gossip, the situation becomes even less rewarding.

One of the charges made against President Arthur was that he supported the so-called Patronage System that allowed an elected official to give favorable jobs to his friends and supporters.

A LASTING MEMORIAL

President Arthur grew increasingly weary as he attempted to ward off attacks by his political foes. Eventually, it became too great of a challenge, and his half-hearted campaign for re-election fell short.

During his time in office, President Arthur contacted the pastor of St. John's Episcopal Church and arranged to purchase a stained-glass window to be placed on the south side of the church. According to the Reverend Peter Larsen, former assistant minister of St. John's, the president, each evening, would sit in the White House, look across Lafayette Square, and see the light of the church shining through that window.

This may have been the only real source of comfort Chester Arthur had as president.

HIGHLIGHTS OF THE ADMINISTRATION OF CHESTER ALAN ARTHUR

- 1882—The Exclusion Act, first general federal immigration law is passed.

- 1882—Chinese Exclusion Act forbids Chinese laborers from entering America.

- 1882—Polygamy is outlawed by U.S. Congress.

- 1883—Pendleton Act is passed and establishes a bipartisan Civil Service Commission.

- 1884—Arthur is defeated in his bid for reelection by Grover Cleveland.

- 1885—Arthur's last official act is to dedicate the Washington Monument.

STEPHEN GROVER CLEVELAND (1837–1908)

State Born: New Jersey   Occupation: Lawyer

Party: Democrat   Religion: Presbyterian

STEPHEN GROVER CLEVELAND

TWENTY-SECOND PRESIDENT
1885–1889

TWENTY-FOURTH PRESIDENT
1893–1897

I have always felt that my training as a minister's son has been more valuable to me as a strengthening influence than any other incident in my life.

—GROVER CLEVELAND, 1853

His résumé includes the following:
- Physically unattractive
- A former hangman
- Father of an illegitimate child
- When forty-nine years old, married his twenty-one-year-old ward

These are hardly the credentials for a presidential candidate. Yet, Stephen Grover Cleveland was elected president not just once, but twice, and he served as our nation's twenty-second and twenty-fourth presidents. He was the only one in history to serve two nonconsecutive terms.

EARLY RELIGIOUS TEACHINGS

Cleveland's entire life was surrounded by religion in one way or another. As the son of a Presbyterian minister, he learned very early in life the familiar Bible stories, as well as the accounts of church heroes such as John Calvin and John Knox. Biographer Robert McElroy writes that his early training "inevitably tended to produce a keen sense of personal responsibility, to make trustworthy character. . . . It taught that there is a right which is eternally right, and a wrong which must be forever wrong."

After his father's death, the most influential preacher for the young Cleveland was the legendary Henry Ward Beecher. After hearing Beecher at Plymouth Church in Brooklyn, New York, Cleveland declared sometime later, "He captured my youthful understanding."

RISE OF A POLITICAL CAREER

As he ascended the political ladder, Cleveland rose from sheriff of Erie County, New York, where he actually sprang the trap for the execution of two prisoners, to mayor of Buffalo and on to governor of New York, all the while relying upon the simple faith taught to him as a young boy.

"Do you know that if Mother were alive," he wrote to his brother, William, a Presbyterian minister, "I should feel so much safer? I have always thought her prayers had so much to do with my success. I shall expect you to help me in that way."

As president, he didn't shed this heritage. At both his inaugurations, he took the oath of office while placing his left hand on a Bible inscribed, *To my son, Stephen Grover Cleveland, from his loving Mother.* The Bible was turned open to Psalm 112, which begins, "Praise ye the LORD. Blessed is the man that feareth the LORD, that delighteth greatly in his commandments." In his second inaugural address on March 4, 1893, he expounded on this thought when he concluded, "Above all, I know there is a Supreme Being who rules the affairs of men and whose goodness and mercy have always followed the American people, and I know He will not turn from us now if we humbly and reverently seek His powerful aid."

SOME SCANDALS

His fathering an illegitimate child created some zesty talk around those Washington circles noted for gossip, but Cleveland was able to weather the storm of wagging tongues, and he gave financial support for the child and its mother.

Nonetheless, it provided ammunition for his enemies.

In the election of 1884—one filled with personal attacks by both sides—Cleveland's Republican opponent, James G. Blaine, urged his supporters to attend political rallies for the Democrat nominee Cleveland. He had them gather at the back of the crowd and chant: "Ma, Ma, Where's my Pa? Gone to the White House. Ha, ha, ha."

Cleveland was able to weather the storm of wagging tongues and won the election.

On June 2, 1886, the president raised more eyebrows when he married Frances Folsom, his twenty-one-year-old ward. It was the only marriage of a president held in the White House. Officiating at the ceremony was the Reverend Byron Suderland of the National Presbyterian Church, which both the president and his young bride attended. "Uncle Cleve" had been her legal guardian since she was eleven.

AN UNHAPPY SECOND TERM

Bitter disputes and setbacks in the national economy, marked by the Depression of 1893, made Grover Cleveland's second term in office less than enjoyable. "I am honest and sincere in my desire to do well," he said, "but the question is whether I know enough to accomplish what I desire." After his retirement to Princeton, New Jersey, he received, once again, the admiration of the public.

On June 24, 1908, as he lay dying, Cleveland summed up his life and beliefs by his last words: "I have tried so hard to do right."

HIGHLIGHTS OF THE ADMINISTRATION OF STEPHEN GROVER CLEVELAND

- 1886—Presidential Succession Act is passed.
- 1886—Apache Wars of New Mexico and Arizona end with the surrender of Geronimo.
- 1887—Antipolygamy Act is signed.
- 1894—Pullman Strike temporarily disrupts rail service.
- 1896—Utah becomes a state.

BENJAMIN HARRISON (1833–1901)

State Born: Ohio   Occupation: Lawyer

Party: Republican   Religion: Presbyterian

BENJAMIN HARRISON

TWENTY-THIRD PRESIDENT

1889–1893

It is a great comfort to trust God—even if his providence is unfavorable.
Prayer steadies one when he is walking in slippery places—
even if things asked for are not given.

—BENJAMIN HARRISON,
in a letter to his son, Russell

Theodore Roosevelt called him "a cold-blooded, narrow-minded, prejudiced, obstinate, timid old psalm-singing Indianapolis politician."

While the first few charges are subject to debate, the latter accusation is not, for Benjamin Harrison centered his social life in the church—the Presbyterian Church, to be exact. He served as a deacon, an elder, and at times, a lay preacher. To Harrison, the church was more than a building or an organization; it was a vital dimension of his life.

EARLY BIBLE READINGS

Almost from the day he was born on the farm of his famous grandfather (President William Henry Harrison) in North Bend, Ohio, young Benjamin was immersed in religious instruction—family prayers, hymn singing, and Bible reading. He attended the Presbyterian-founded Miami University in Oxford, Ohio, where he met his future bride, Caroline (Carrie) Scott, the daughter of a Presbyterian minister.

At college, Harrison was torn between two professions: theology and law. He chose the latter on the conviction that this country needed more Christian lawyers, while at the same time remaining a staunch supporter of the church.

The Centennial Memorial Publication from the First Presbyterian Church in Indianapolis, Indiana (the church he and his wife attended after he moved there to practice law in 1854), recalls young Harrison's enthusiasm:

> When he came to this place, he lost no time in uniting with the church and taking up such work as he found to do. He became a teacher in the Sabbath school, he was constant in his attendance. . . .
> His voice was heard in prayer meetings . . . and, whether public or private, he gave testimony for his faith and the lordship of his Master.

His law practice was interrupted by the Civil War. Young Harrison served as an officer with the Union Army and at the war's end, Brigadier General Harrison returned to his law practice with thoughts of running for public office.

"He who wears worthily the honors of the church of Christ cannot fail," wrote Harrison's father in a letter of encouragement, "to be the worthy recipient of the honors of this country. Would to God that more of our officeholders were God-fearing men!"

An Unexpected Political Career

He didn't sound or look much like a politician, but the stout, five-foot-six-inch bearded, patriarchal candidate was elected to the United States Senate in 1881. Seven years later, he was the surprise Republican candidate for president.

Even more surprisingly, he won the election, although not by popular vote. He received nearly 100,000 fewer votes than incumbent Grover Cleveland. Nevertheless, he won the electoral vote 233-168. He was not one who might be deemed "a people's president."

Biographer Glenn Kittler described Harrison as "a cold, aloof man, unapproachable and rather dull . . . a family man, a religious man, a temperate man, and if he did nothing, at least he kept us out of trouble."

On the other side of the coin, Harrison earned a solid reputation for opposing corrupt politicians and the famous spoils system in which jobs are given out to family, friends, and supporters of the winning candidate for election.

The Shocking Death of His Wife

The unexpected death of his wife just two weeks before the election of 1892 left Harrison in shock, unable to complete his campaign. This tragedy, coupled with the fact that he never gained the confidence of the electorate, contributed to his defeat by his old foe, Grover Cleveland.

After retirement from the hectic Washington scene, Benjamin Harrison returned to private life, serving as an elder in his church in Indianapolis.

Prior to his death in 1901, Harrison urged others to call upon the powers of God during the times of personal crisis. When, for example, his son (Russell) faced financial woes, Harrison gave this fatherly advice: "Prayer steadies one when he is walking in slippery places."

HIGHLIGHTS OF THE ADMINISTRATION OF BENJAMIN HARRISON

- 1889—First Pan-American Congress is held.
- 1889—Oklahoma Territory is opened for settlement.
- 1889—North Dakota, South Dakota, Montana and Washington become states.
- 1890—Wyoming and Idaho become states.
- 1892—Harrison is defeated in his bid for reelection by former President Grover Cleveland.

WILLIAM MCKINLEY (1843–1901)

State Born: Ohio   Occupation: Lawyer

Party: Republican   Religion: Methodist

WILLIAM
MCKINLEY

TWENTY-FIFTH PRESIDENT
1897–1901

Nearer, my God to Thee,
Nearer to Thee!
E'en thought it be a cross
That raiseth me;
Still all my song shall be,
Nearer, my God, to Thee,
Nearer, my God, to Thee,
Nearer to Thee!

—Text of President McKinley's favorite hymn

It was springtime 1853 in Poland, Ohio, a small hamlet a few miles south of Youngstown. Budding flowers displayed signs of new life. Inside the town's Methodist Church, a revivalist talked about another kind of new life. To the front of the church marched a ten-year-old lad who asked to become a probationary member. Forty-three years later, this young man would be elected twenty-fifth president of the United States.

From that spring day until he died, William McKinley kept a close affiliation with the Methodist Church. "My belief," he wrote in 1899, "embraces the Divinity of Christ and a recognition of Christianity as the mightiest factor in the world's civilization." He embraced Christianity, specifically Methodism, with a fervor few could equal.

When he opened his law practice in Canton, Ohio, McKinley joined the First Methodist Episcopal Church and served as its Sunday school superintendent.

PERSONAL TRAGEDY

McKinley and his wife, Ida, had two children, both of whom died (one was four years old; the other, four months). The shock and grief were too much for the mother, and she suffered a nervous breakdown. She never recovered and remained an invalid tormented by epilepsy.

Afraid to leave his wife alone, McKinley cared for all her needs. When he ran for the presidency in 1896, he refused to tour the country and chose, instead, to conduct his campaign from the front porch of his home in Canton. After he defeated William Jennings Bryan and moved to 1600 Pennsylvania Avenue, McKinley continued to maintain his personal care of his wife. Protocol called for the First Lady to sit with the other wives at official functions, but the president insisted that she sit with him. His devotion to her remained to his last breath.

While president, McKinley attended the Metropolitan Methodist Church in Washington, D.C., and like former president Hayes, invited friends and members of Congress for Sunday-evening hymn sings in the White House.

A WAR WITH A MISSIONARY PURPOSE

On April 11, 1898, President McKinley declared war with Spain. It turned out to be a 113-day skirmish and, in the peace treaty, America acquired some Pacific territories, including the Philippines.

When the Filipinos revolted against American rule, McKinley concluded, "There was nothing left for us to do but to take them all, and educate the Filipinos, and uplift and civilize and Christianize them."

Assassination

On September 6, 1901, less than one year after his election to a second term, the president stood in a long receiving line at the Pan-American Exposition in Buffalo, New York. The afternoon before, he had received a thunderous ovation for a speech that concluded, "Our earnest prayer is that God will graciously vouchsafe prosperity, happiness, and peace to all our neighbors, and like blessings to all peoples and powers on earth." This day, the people pressed forward to meet him in person.

One of the greeters was a young man with a bandaged hand. His name was Leon Czolgosz, an anarchist. When the two were less than a foot apart, Czolgosz fired two shots from a pistol that was hidden by the bandages. The president reeled and slumped backwards into the arms of a Secret Service agent. As other Secret Service agents subdued Czolgosz, President McKinley lay on the ground. He whispered to reporters, "My wife . . . be careful how you tell her—oh, be careful!"

Eight days later, the president said, "It is useless, gentlemen. I think we ought to have prayer." He then turned to his wife, and whispered, "It is God's way. His will, not ours, be done."

President McKinley's last audible sounds before lapsing into a final coma on September 14, 1901, were the words to that favorite hymn often sung on Sundays in the White House: "Nearer, My God, to Thee."

HIGHLIGHTS OF THE ADMINISTRATION OF WILLIAM McKINLEY

- 1898—United States proposes "neutral intervention" of Cuba that leads to the Hundred-Day War.

- 1900—McKinley wins reelection to a second term.

- 1900—Congress adopts the Gold Standard Act.

- 1901—McKinley is assassinated.

THEODORE ROOSEVELT (1858–1919)

State Born: New York   Occupation: Writer/Politician

Party: Republican   Religion: Reformed

THEODORE
ROOSEVELT

TWENTY-SIXTH PRESIDENT

1901–1909

The religious man who is most useful is not he whose sole care is to save his own soul, but the man whose religion bids him strive to advance decency and clean living and to make the world a better place for his fellows to live in.

—THEODORE ROOSEVELT

The conservation of natural resources is the fundamental problem."
No, this is not a press release by the Department of Environmental Resources. This timely warning was written by Theodore Roosevelt in 1891 and came out of his Presbyterian and Reformed conviction that the natural resources of the world were given by God to humankind with the admonition to take care of them.

But Roosevelt's religious heritage produced more than lip service. The Rough Rider was another of our presidents who attended church regularly and stoutly supported the practice, declaring, "I know all the excuses for not going to church. I know that one can worship the Creator and dedicate himself to good living in a grove of trees or by a

127

running brook or in one's own house, just as well as in church. But I also know that, as a matter of cold fact, the average man does not thus worship or dedicate himself."

HIS REFORMED TRADITION

The Roosevelt family was steeped in the Reformed tradition, and young Theodore joined that church when he was sixteen years old. He never wavered from it, which resulted in a minor crisis during his undergraduate days at Harvard. For more than three years, Roosevelt had taught Sunday school at Christ Episcopal Church near the campus. When the rector discovered Theodore was not an Episcopalian, he asked him to join the congregation. "No," said the young man. "I'm Reformed now, and will be when I die." The rector dismissed him instantly.

During his presidency, Teddy Roosevelt maintained his support of the Reformed Church. He was so consistently punctual when attending Grace Reformed Church at Fifteenth and G streets, NW, that members set their watches on his arrival for the eleven o'clock Sunday worship. One Sunday he was late, causing everything to be upset. After the service, Roosevelt sought out the head usher, D. O. Thomas, and apologized, promising that he would never be late again. He kept his word.

A REGULAR WORSHIPER WHO MADE HIS PRESENCE KNOWN

Roosevelt took part in the services with the same infectious enthusiasm that characterized his other activities. He was a particularly vigorous but raspy hymn singer, especially during his favorite hymns, "How Firm a Foundation" and "A Mighty Fortress Is Our God." Worshipers reported that his voice could be heard above the rest of the congregation.

One popular story of the day had Roosevelt reorganizing the heavenly choir after his death with ten thousand sopranos, ten thousand altos, and ten thousand tenors, adding, "I'll sing bass."

He was sensitive to the charge that church people frequently were hypocritical in their everyday lives. At the dedication of Grace Church in 1903, Roosevelt warned, "We must, in our lives, in our efforts, endeavor to further the cause of brotherhood in the human family; and we must do it in such a way that the men anxious to find subject for complaint or derision in the churches . . . may not be able to find it by pointing out any contrast between our profession and our lives."

A "Muscular Christianity"

The tendency of members of one denomination to dispute those of another aroused Roosevelt's ire. "I wish," he said, "I could make every member of a Christian church feel that just insofar as he spends his time in quarreling with other Christians of other churches, he is helping discredit Christianity in the eyes of the world. Avoid as you would the plague those who seek to embroil you in conflict, one Christian sect with another."

Author John Sutherland Bonnell called Teddy Roosevelt's faith a "muscular Christianity," which just about says it all. He projected an uninhibited masculine image throughout all of his life. At the same time, he disdained dirty jokes and avoided anyone who began telling one. He felt that he had the right to live as his conscience dictated— in an "unpolluted environment."

Faith without Works Is Dead

The president's self-determination led him to reject some of the more orthodox teachings of early twentieth-century Christianity, among which was the doctrine of the salvation by faith, as promoted by the Lutherans and Presbyterians. "I believe in the gospel of works as put down in the Epistle of James—"Be ye doers of the word, and not hearers only.'" He also trumpeted another theme found in the same epistle: "Faith without works is dead."

His favorite text, Micah 6:8, reinforced this theme: "He hath shewed thee, O man, what is good; and what doth the LORD require of thee, but to do justly, and to love mercy, and to walk humbly with thy God?"

PUSHING THE ENVELOPE

Self-determined? Definitely! But there were times when Teddy Roosevelt's individualistic zeal to push the envelope drew a less than enthusiastic response. For example, he set Washington tongues wagging when he invited a black man, the famous educator Booker T. Washington, to dinner at the White House. No president before him had ever invited a nonwhite to share dinner at the Executive Mansion, but Roosevelt believed that the proclamation, "All men are created equal," was more than an ideal written on parchment.

There was one event, however, which proved to be a hurdle that even the Rough Rider found difficult to conquer. In fact, it was a political disaster that nearly conquered him. In 1905, the president assigned Augustus Saint-Gaudens, an American sculptor, to design a new penny, along with ten- and twenty-dollar gold pieces. Saint-Gaudens recommended (for purely aesthetic reasons) to eliminate the words "In God We Trust," calling the inscription an "inartistic intrusion." The president concurred and ordered the words removed. The new coins were minted and issued in November 1907.

Judging from the avalanche of criticism, one might conclude that the president had vetoed a bill favoring motherhood and apple pie. The *New York Sun* lambasted the coins as examples of "modern barbarism." Representative Morris Sheppard (Democrat, Texas) deplored the "godless coinage." One caustic soul suggested that perhaps the president wished the inscription to read "In Theodore we trust," and to replace the symbol of the eagle with the teddy bear, named after Roosevelt.

When Congress passed a bill to restore the inscription after July 1, 1908, the president offered no veto. He no doubt, also, breathed a heavy sigh of relief.

Perhaps the historian and journalist Henry R. Luce best put into perspective President Theodore Roosevelt's individualistic theology in perspective: "My own political hero was Theodore Roosevelt, who fallible though he was, did not hesitate to assert that righteousness is relevant to politics and all the public affairs of men and nations."

HIGHLIGHTS OF THE ADMINISTRATION OF THEODORE ROOSEVELT

- 1903—Construction begins on the Panama Canal.

- 1903—Wright brothers make the first successful powered airplane flight.

- 1906—Roosevelt forces the Hepburn Act that strengthens railroad regulations.

- 1906—Roosevelt is awarded the Nobel Peace Prize.

- 1907—Oklahoma becomes a state.

- 1908—The Model T is introduced.

WILLIAM HOWARD TAFT (1857–1930)

State Born: Ohio   Occupation: Lawyer

Party: Republican   Religion: Unitarian

WILLIAM HOWARD TAFT

TWENTY-SEVENTH PRESIDENT

1909–1913

I am a Unitarian. I believe in God. I do not believe in the divinity of Christ, and there are other of the postulates of the orthodox creed to which I cannot subscribe.

—WILLIAM HOWARD TAFT

He didn't want to be president, and he sounded like it. He didn't want to be a Christian, and he let that be known also.

In stark contrast to his predecessor, William Howard Taft boldly declared a kind of faith that chafed with the mainstream of early twentieth-century American thinking. "I am a Unitarian. I believe in God. I do *not* believe in the divinity of Christ, and there are other of the postulates of the orthodox creed to which I cannot subscribe."

CRITICISM FOR HIS FAITH

Taft was put to the test when, in 1899, he was offered the position as president of Yale, the school he loved so dearly. He refused the appointment on the basis that his convictions were not in harmony with the orthodox Congregational spirit of his alma mater.

While such honesty may be admired from a distance of time, it served as fodder for Taft's political enemies. "Think of the United States with a president who does not believe that Jesus Christ was the Son of God," exclaimed one critic, "but looks upon our immaculate Savior as a common bastard and low cunning impostor!" Taft, however, was willing to take his chances and threw down the gauntlet. "If the American electorate is so narrow not to elect a Unitarian, well and good," he said. "I can stand it."

Obviously, Taft's concern was unwarranted. This six-foot, three-hundred-pound candidate won election to the presidential office by more than one million votes over William Jennings Bryan, nick-named the Silver-Tongued Orator, who was an outspoken Christian fundamentalist. Years later, Bryan would gain further notoriety as the prosecutor and star witness in the famous Monkey Trial of John Scopes in Dayton, Tennessee.

THE QUESTION AT HIS INAUGURATION

Yet the issue of William Howard Taft's religion still disquieted many Christians. Rumors circulated after the election that, because of his Unitarian views, the president-elect would be unable to swear his oath of office on a Bible—a tradition established by George Washington.

On March 4, 1909, because a strong blizzard had dropped four inches of snow on Washington the night before, the Inauguration ceremony was moved indoors to the Senate room of the Capitol. The chaplain of the Senate, the Reverend Everett Hale (author of such stories as "The Man Without a Country"), led the assembled gathering in praying aloud the Lord's Prayer. There is no report available as to whether or not Taft joined in.

For many of the onlookers, the question yet to be answered was, would the president take the oath of office on a Bible?

The moment of truth was at hand. Escorted by Senator Philander Knox, Taft approached Chief Justice Melville Fuller who presented him with a Bible. The president-elect extended his left hand and placed it solidly on the leather cover. The crowd murmured and then became silent. The oath was administered, and the new president added, "So help me God." Then he took the Bible in both hands and kissed it.

The few who were able to attend the ceremony burst into a spontaneous applause that lasted for several minutes. In order to accommodate more people, the president moved the rest of the inauguration into the House of Representatives where he delivered a long address ending with a plea for "the aid of Almighty God in the discharge of my responsible duties."

The skeptics appeared to be satisfied—at least for the present.

The *Washington Star* of Monday, March 7, 1909, reported that the president spent his first Sunday in office attending All Souls' Unitarian Church and in relaxation with members of his family. No visitors were allowed; no business was conducted. The Sabbath was declared a day of rest by and for the president.

HIS RELIGION BECAME HIS DOWNFALL

But Sundays were about the only days of rest for President Taft during the next few years. Splits within the party coupled with growing criticism of his so-called infidel religious views, created tension between the White House and the electorate. He certainly did not help his cause when he ruffled a few feathers just before the election of 1912. At a time when the majority of American citizens viewed the Roman Catholic Church with suspicion, the president said, "I believe the Catholic Church to be one of the bulwarks against socialism and anarchy in this country, and I welcome its presence here."

President Taft's loss of the election of 1912 to Woodrow Wilson may have been due in part to his disregard for political diplomacy. "Taft meant well," said Theodore Roosevelt, "but he meant well feebly."

Speaker of the House Joseph Cannon put it more bluntly: "The trouble with Taft is that if he were Pope, he would think it necessary to appoint a few Protestant cardinals."

In 1921, when President Warren G. Harding selected him chief justice of the Supreme Court, former president Taft was in his glory. "In my present life," he said, "I don't remember I was ever president."

HIGHLIGHTS OF THE ADMINISTRATION OF WILLIAM HOWARD TAFT

- 1909—Taft fails in his attempt to revise protective tariff.

- 1910—Republican unity suffers and proves to be the start of the Bull Moose Party.

- 1911—The Roosevelt Dam is completed.

- 1912—New Mexico and Arizona become states.

- 1913—Henry Ford develops an automobile assembly line.

THOMAS WOODROW WILSON (1856–1924)

State Born: Virginia   Occupation:
Party: Democrat   Lawyer/Educator
                                        Religion: Presbyterian

THOMAS WOODROW WILSON

TWENTY-EIGHTH PRESIDENT

1913–1921

Why has Jesus Christ so far not succeeded in inducing the world to follow his teachings? I am proposing a practical scheme to carry out His aims.

—WOODROW WILSON, 1919

Can a president be *too* God-centered?

Ask a conservative fundamentalist, and he'll immediately respond, "Certainly not!" A liberal might ponder the question for a while, whereas someone like Sigmund Freud would venture to say, "Definitely." In fact, that's exactly what he *did* say. In his analysis of Woodrow Wilson, the legendary psychoanalyst contended that in his own mind, the twenty-eighth president believed himself akin to Jesus the Christ.

Thomas Woodrow Wilson, so characterized by Dr. Freud, was the son of a Presbyterian minister, whom he often referred to as "my incomparable father." The young Wilson was schooled in both sacred and secular studies, pursuing the gamut of the academic field from doctoral student of history at Johns Hopkins to a university professorship and the presidency of Princeton University.

Through all of his academic pursuits, Wilson clung to a solid and uncompromising faith that left little room for debate. "So far as religion is concerned," he said, "argument is adjourned."

Each day of his adult life was accompanied by morning and evening prayers as well as Bible readings. Freud noted that the president "wore out two or three Bibles in the course of his life."

PREDESTINATION WAS CENTRAL TO HIS FAITH

Deeply imbedded in President Wilson's theology was a full acceptance of the Calvinistic teachings about predestination. When, for example, a national or personal tragedy struck, he would argue, "It's only God's will."

Speaking to black leaders in November 1913, Wilson actually attempted to convince them that their plight was part of God's plan: "Segregation is not humiliating but a benefit, and ought to be so regarded by you gentlemen."

When his wife, Ellen, suddenly became ill and died while he was in the White House in 1914, the president, believing that such fate was a punishment for sin, sat beside her body for two full days. He stared into space, spoke to no one, and according to some close friends, came near to having a nervous breakdown.

Once in a while, Wilson received comfort from his views on predestination. "I believe in Divine Providence," he confessed. "If I did not, I would go crazy."

Afraid for Wilson's emotional state following the death of his wife, friends of the president arranged a meeting with the beautiful widow, Edith Galt. A whirlwind courtship followed, which led to their marriage in 1915. "She was sent to me by God," said Wilson.

President Wilson won reelection in 1916, campaigning on the slogan, "He kept us out of war!" Ironically, one month after his second inauguration, he took America into World War I.

Our First Woman President

It was during his second term in office that something happened that would change not only the ability of the president to fulfill his responsibilities, but also open the door to a future possible political breakthrough. President Wilson was crippled by a massive stroke that left his entire left side paralyzed and his speech garbled. According to reliable historical records, it was Mrs. Wilson who handled the affairs of state. Many astute historians have concluded that Edith Galt Wilson, in reality, was our nation's first woman president.

The frustration of his illness, plus a series of political setbacks (including the unwillingness of the United States to support the League of Nations for which he had fought vigorously), turned President Wilson into a defeated man. "You can't fight God," he quietly said.

After he left the White House, the former president, on rare occasions, displayed some of his old fighting spirit. On Armistice Day, 1923, he struck a positive chord for predestination. "I cannot refrain from saying it. I am not one of those who have the least anxiety about the triumph of the principles I have stood for. I have seen fools resist Providence before and I have seen their destruction, as will come upon these again—utter destruction and contempt. That we shall prevail is as sure as that God reigns."

For the most part, however, the twenty-eighth president lived his last days in loneliness and bitterness. "I'm just tired of swimming upstream," he often told his friends.

Now, what would Sigmund Freud have said about that?

HIGHLIGHTS OF THE ADMINISTRATION OF WOODROW WILSON

- 1913—United States establishes a graduated federal income tax.

- 1914—Federal Trade Commission is established.

- 1914—World War I begins in Europe.

- 1914—The Panama Canal is opened.

- 1916—Child labor is prohibited by law.

- 1917—United States enters World War I.

- 1918—Wilson delivers his Fourteen Points speech to Congress.

- 1918—Armistice is signed with Germany.

- 1919—The Eighteenth Amendment is ratified, which results in the start of prohibition.

- 1919—Wilson suffers a catastrophic, disabling stroke.

- 1920—The Nineteenth Amendment is ratified, giving women the right to vote.

WARREN GAMALIEL HARDING (1865–1923)

State Born: Ohio

Party: Republican

Occupation: Newspaper

Editor/Publisher

Religion: Baptist

WARREN GAMALIEL HARDING

TWENTY-NINTH PRESIDENT

1921–1923

If you will talk to God about me everyday by name and ask Him somehow to give me strength for my great task, I will be thankful beyond words.

—WARREN G. HARDING,
*request of a friend just prior to
his inauguration in 1921*

In 1921, for the first time in history, American women were allowed to vote in a presidential election. As a result, they helped elect a six-foot, white-haired, superbly handsome Ohio native, Warren G. Harding, who resembled a matinee idol and carried himself with Washingtonian dignity and nobility.

The first newspaper publisher to be elected to the presidency was not your typical politician. He seemed to be a "Main Streeter" to the American public. He loved poker, golf, and baseball. Instead of barnstorming the country on a whistle-stop tour, Warren Harding conducted his famous "front porch campaign" from his white-frame house in Marion, Ohio. It was this simplistic approach to life that echoed his campaign theme for a return to "normalcy" and swept him into office in 1920 in a landslide election.

A Simple Faith

Even Harding's personal faith reflected the simple, down-home philosophy that appealed to the majority of the electorate. "What doth the Lord require of thee, but to do justly, and to love mercy, and to walk humbly with thy God?" he asked, quoting from Micah 6:8.

Some of his other attributes may not have been as politically advantageous. His physical attractiveness provoked gossip in vulnerable Washington social circles. President Harding, since age twenty-six, was married to Florence nee' Kling, an astute businesswoman, who was divorced (a very negative part of anyone's resume at this time) and was five years his senior (another fact that raised an eyebrow or two within polite society). However, President Harding appeared to have a difficult time with the monogamy expectation in marriage. So-called inside observers whispered stories about the president's numerous alleged love affairs.

The partners in his alleged extracurricular activities included a close friend's wife—Nan Britton, a beautiful blonde—who reportedly bore his illegitimate daughter. He was also infamous for hosting liquor-filled poker parties at the White House. On occasion, when he was low on cash, the president was said to wager even individual pieces of fine White House china. As a result, several pieces of the china collection remain lost to this day. Even famous newspaper editor, William Allen White wrote, "What a story! The story of Babylon is a Sunday school story compared with the story of Washington from June 1919 to July 1923."

President Harding countered with a pronouncement that could have been taken from the book of a traveling evangelist: "It is my conviction, that the fundamental trouble with the people of the

United States is that they have gotten too far away from Almighty God."

The tactic worked. President Harding did not lose public support due to his indiscretions (real or imagined). Instead, the distinguished-looking Ohioan remained extremely popular. He was indeed a "people's president" who, unlike his predecessor, identified with the average citizen and was never hesitant to call upon the best minds of the day to advise him.

A DIFFERENT SOURCE FOR HOPE

Many biographers attempt to paint a portrait of President Harding as a man with a deep, personal faith. However, as they are quick to admit, he rarely showed any outward signs of it. In reality, it appeared as though Harding considered American business as our ultimate hope. "American business," he claimed, "is not a monster, but an expression of God-given impulse to create, and the savior of our happiness."

A SUSPICIOUS DEATH

The life of this most colorful character came to an abrupt end on August 2, 1923.

What exactly caused his unexpected death will probably remain a mystery, for eyewitness reports vary. Some accounts say that the president suffered a sudden heart attack while delivering a speech in Seattle, Washington; other authorities conclude that death resulted from a few days later from an advanced case of pneumonia. Others insist that President Harding's demise resulted from ptomaine poisoning on a train. Some went so far as to speculate that he was poisoned by his wife, Florence (whom the president affectionately called "Duchess"), who feared that the president's lifestyle was about to bring disgrace and possible impeachment. In the eyes of many, her refusal to permit an autopsy supported this theory.

Whatever the cause of the president's death, the news came as a shock. Citizens throughout the United States, especially the women, openly wept.

HIGHLIGHTS OF THE ADMINISTRATION OF WARREN GAMALIEL HARDING

- 1921—Peace is declared between Germany and Austria.

- 1922—The Teapot Dome Scandal becomes news.

- 1923—President Harding dies mysteriously aboard a train.

JOHN CALVIN COOLIDGE

State Born: Vermont   Occupation: Lawyer

Party: Republican   Religion: Congregational

JOHN
CALVIN COOLIDGE

THIRTIETH PRESIDENT

1923–1929

*The higher state to which she [America] seeks the allegiance of all mankind is
not human but of Divine origin. She cherishes no purpose save to merit the
favor of Almighty God.*

—CALVIN COOLIDGE,
inaugural address, 1925

William Allen White described him as "a Puritan in Babylon."

It was the time of the Roaring Twenties, when Eliot Ness and the Charleston were household words, and people sang "Yankee Doodle Dandy." The stock market was going up while morality was going down. The Teapot Dome Scandal was rocking Capitol Hill.

Into this den of lions marched President John Calvin Coolidge, who gained a reputation as a rigidly moral and an uncompromisingly honest soul who held his tongue and kept to himself. The reporters dubbed him Silent Cal.

One popular story, told even to this day, involves the time President Coolidge was sitting at dinner when a fellow guest who was well aware of his reputation for taciturnity attempted to lure him into conversation.

"I have made a bet, Mr. Coolidge," she began, "that I can get more than two words out of you."

Calvin's reply? "You lose."

DRAMATIC CHANGE IN THE OVAL OFFICE

Some observers felt that Coolidge was out of place in this society, while others considered him the muted conscience of the nation. Yet no one could argue the fact that his presence in the Executive Mansion was a dramatic change of pace from the flamboyant nature of the man he followed.

His presidency began shortly after midnight in his father's farmhouse in Plymouth, Vermont, on August 3, 1923. Vice President Calvin Coolidge was abruptly awakened by a loud banging on the front door from a telegram carrier announcing that President Harding was dead, and the vice president was to immediately arrange to be sworn into office.

Coolidge asked his father, a notary, to prepare for the administration of the presidential oath. He went upstairs to dress, but before coming downstairs, he went to his knees in prayer.

Shortly thereafter, in a room lit by kerosene lamps, Calvin Coolidge placed his hand on a Bible formerly owned by his deceased mother, and he took the oath of office from the senior Coolidge, becoming the only president inaugurated by his father.

On the first Sunday after reaching Washington, D.C., President Coolidge and wife, Grace, attended worship services at First Congregational Church. Although they both attended this church as a regular habit, neither chose to become a member.

The Purpose of the Church

President Coolidge—laconic, aloof, and a loner—was simple in life and simple in his faith. He felt that preaching should be limited to the standard themes: "salvation by grace," "a change of heart," or "the power of prayer." He became highly suspicious of clergymen who spoke in support of the budding "social gospel." He said, "I wouldn't for a minute be critical of the church and its work, but I think most of the clergy today are preaching socialism."

In the eyes of President Coolidge, the church had a fundamental obligation to lead our nation. "America," he said in his 1925 inauguration address, "seeks no earthly empire built on blood and force. No ambition, no temptation lures her to thought of foreign dominions. The legions which she sends forth are armed, not with the sword, but with the cross."

If Frances Bacon was correct when he wrote, "No pleasure is comparable to the standing upon the vantage ground of truth," Calvin Coolidge must have been the happiest man on earth, or at least he tried to be. He loved to seek the truth, and he pitied those who failed to recognize it. In his autobiography, Coolidge wrote, "For a man not to recognize the truth . . . is for him to be at war with his own nature, to commit suicide. That is why 'the wages of sin is death.'"

Although he was known for his reserve, the president did speak forcefully when the occasion called for it. In his autobiography, for example, he observed that anyone accepting the challenge to serve the nation as president of the United States must "realize, with an increasing sense of humility, that he is but an instrument in the hands of God."

For a quiet Puritan, that's saying an awful lot.

HIGHLIGHTS OF THE ADMINISTRATION
OF JOHN CALVIN COOLIDGE

- 1923—Coolidge calls for a policy of isolation for the United States.

- 1924—The first presidential campaign in which radio was used extensively.

- 1924—Coolidge is elected to his first full term as president.

- 1927—The Paris Peace Pact was signed.

- 1928—Coolidge chooses not to run for reelection.

HERBERT CLARK HOOVER (1874–1964)

State Born: Iowa

Party: Republican

Occupation: Engineer

Religion: Society of Friends
(Quaker)

HERBERT CLARK HOOVER

THIRTY-FIRST PRESIDENT

1929–1933

*Bert can take it better than most people, because he has deeply ingrained in
him the Quaker feeling that nothing matters if you are "right with God."*

—MRS. HERBERT (LOU) HOOVER,
*explaining the president's calm reaction
to his critics during the Depression*

I come from Quaker stock. My ancestors were persecuted for their
beliefs. Here they sought and found religious freedom. By blood and
conviction I stand for religious tolerance both in act and in spirit. The
glory of our American ideals is the right of every man to worship God
according to the dictates of his own conscience."

These were the words of Herbert Clark Hoover in his acceptance
speech for nomination as president of the United States on August
11, 1928. It was a significant statement for the Republican nominee,
since the campaign of that year would have religion as one of its
primary issues.

CAMPAIGN AND THE ROMAN CATHOLIC QUESTION

Hoover's Democratic opponent, New York's Governor Alfred Smith, was an Irish Roman Catholic. Many Hoover supporters suggested out loud that a Roman Catholic in the White House would mean the surrender of power by the federal government to the pope in Rome. A lot of people accepted this theory. With the aid of this fear in the hearts of American Protestant voters, Herbert Hoover won by a landslide, carrying forty of the forty-eight states. Smith, on the other hand, even failed to win his own state.

INSTANT PROBLEMS

The honeymoon was short-lived. The stock market crash of October 1929 was blamed largely on President Hoover. Shantytowns that sprung up around the country were dubbed "Hoovervilles," and broken-down automobiles were called "Hoover wagons." Empty pockets turned inside out emphasized "Hoover flags," for to Hooverize, meant to economize.

SOME BOLD STANDS

Yet the man who campaigned with the slogan "Two chickens in every pot and a car in every garage" seemed to take it all in stride and refused to knuckle under. When he invited the wife of a black congressman to join other congressional wives for tea, he was criticized by the southern press for "defiling the White House." Hoover countered by inviting the president of Tuskegee Institute and boldly declared that the White House would be "defiled" several times during his administration.

The president, who declared in his inaugural address of March 4, 1929, that "only through the guidance of Almighty Providence can I hope to discharge [the Presidency's] ever-increasing burdens," often attended the meetings of the Religious Society of Friends in Washington, D.C., where the challenge "I mind the light—dost thou?" is inscribed on a sundial in the garden. Here, like others of his faith, he sought to respond to that challenge and seek assurance from the "inner light" in all dimensions of life.

He needed that assurance, especially when he lost his bid for reelection in 1932 to then governor of New York, Franklin D. Roosevelt, who promised Americans a "new deal." Hoover left office under a very dark cloud.

In the years that followed, at no time did Hoover lash out at the people for their misunderstanding. Instead, he retired in typical Quaker fashion and waited in silence.

His patience was rewarded. Before his death at ninety years of age, he had regained the trust and affection of America. President Harry S Truman (a Democrat), appointed Hoover to chair two national committees and, in 1947, to head the President's Economic Mission to Germany and Austria. Later, in the 1950s and 1960s, he received thunderous ovations from delegates to the Republican national conventions.

One might rightly conclude that Herbert Hoover lived to see the fruits of patient submission to the "inner light."

HIGHLIGHTS OF THE ADMINISTRATION OF HERBERT HOOVER

- 1929—Federal Farm Board is established.

- 1929—Stock market crashes, sending the nation into the Great Depression.

- 1931—"The Star-Spangled Banner" is adopted as the national anthem.

- 1931—The Empire State Building opens in New York City.

- 1931—Reconstruction Finance Corporation is founded.

- 1932—Hoover is defeated in his bid for reelection by Franklin Roosevelt.

FRANKLIN DELANO ROOSEVELT (1882–1945)

State Born: New York

Party: Democrat

Occupation:
Lawyer/Politician

Religion: Episcopalian

FRANKLIN DELANO ROOSEVELT

THIRTY-SECOND PRESIDENT

1933–1945

I feel that a comprehensive study of the Bible is a liberal education for anyone. Nearly all of the great men of our country have been well-versed in the teachings of the Bible.

—FRANKLIN D. ROOSEVELT

I always felt that my husband's religion had something to do with his confidence in himself," wrote Eleanor Roosevelt in her book, *This I Remember.* She related that her husband felt all human beings were given specific tasks to perform here on earth, and with those tasks the ability to accomplish them.

This was not a high-sounding platitude spoken from an ivory tower. Mrs. Roosevelt drew upon firsthand experience after helping her husband fight the dreaded disease polio, which struck him on August 9, 1921.

In what would become known as the typical Roosevelt style, the thirty-nine-year-old politician who had gained national attention in a losing cause as the Democratic Party's vice presidential candidate one year earlier, turned this handicap into an advantage. Astute historian Paul Conkin wrote, "Polio made the aristocrat Roosevelt into an underdog. For him, it replaced the log cabin."

A POLITICAL CAREER BEGINS

Conkin may have been right. Roosevelt won the election as governor of New York in 1928.

Four years later, the reward of his patient struggle surfaced as Franklin Delano Roosevelt, offering a promise of a "new deal for the American people," defeated incumbent Herbert Hoover and became the thirty-second president of the United States by carrying all but six states. It was the first in a series of four consecutive victories—an accomplishment unparalleled by any other president.

Perhaps it was his personal physical struggles, or maybe it was the unstable economy in the country that led the newly elected president to conclude his first inaugural address on March 4, 1933, with the prayer: "In this dedication of a nation we humbly ask the blessing of God. May he protect each and every one of us. May he guide me in the days to come."

During the next twelve years, President Roosevelt depended heavily on that guidance. Overcoming polio and political opponents at the same time requires the inner strength of a self-determined individual. Perhaps it was this inner strength that urged him on to greater heights. "If you have spent two years in bed trying to wiggle your big toe," he said, "then anything else seems easy."

Personal strength notwithstanding, the president was not immune to the encouragement offered through corporate worship. He enjoyed attending church services and became an active leader at St. James Episcopal Church in his hometown, Hyde Park, New York. Later, because of his physical limitations, attendance at church had to be limited to special occasions. Nevertheless, during important happenings, such as inaugurations or whenever a crisis loomed on the horizon (especially during the war years), Roosevelt arranged for private services, whereupon he asked the officiating clergyman to seek the strength and guidance of the Lord.

Two Sources of Strength

President Roosevelt, whose mellow and resonant voice comforted Americans over radio through his "fireside chats," received his strength and comfort from two sources. The first was the Bible, which he read regularly, his favorite sections being Psalm 23, the Beatitudes, and the thirteenth chapter of First Corinthians.

The second was prayer. He emphasized this point in a prayer concluding his second inaugural address in 1937. With the threat of war looming over the horizon, President Roosevelt told an anxious nation, "While this duty rests upon me, I shall do my utmost to speak their purpose and to do their will, seeking divine guidance to help each and every one to give light to them that sit in darkness and to guide our feet into the way of peace."

World War II

That divine guidance was never more important than on the "day of infamy," December 7, 1941, when Americans were thrown headlong into World War II with the bombing of Pearl Harbor by the Japanese.

Coupled with his physical ailments, the strains of the years at war took their toll, and Roosevelt aged rapidly. During the 1944 campaign, his political opponents used his declining health as a major issue. In spite of this, Roosevelt won an easy victory over the Republican nominee, New York governor Thomas E. Dewey.

Like the founders of our nation, President Roosevelt was convinced that the hand of Almighty God was necessary for victory over the enemy. On the day after the D-Day invasion on June 6, 1944, the president offered a public prayer:

Almighty God: Our sons, pride of our nation, this day have set upon a mighty endeavor, a struggle to preserve our Republic, our religion, and our civilization, and to set free a suffering humanity. Lead them straight and true; give strength to their arms, stoutness to their hearts, steadfastness in their faith. They will need thy blessings. Their road will be long and hard, for the enemy is strong. He may hurl back our forces. Success may not come with rushing speed, but we shall return again and again; and we know by thy grace, and by the righteousness of our cause, our sons will triumph.

Some will never return. Embrace these, Father, and receive them, thy heroic servants, into thy kingdom.

And for us at home—fathers, mothers, children, wives, sisters, and brothers of brave men overseas, whose thoughts and prayers are ever with them—help us, Almighty God, to rededicate ourselves in renewed faith in thee in this hour of great sacrifice.

A Shocking Death

On April 12, 1945, while on a working vacation in the "Little White House" at Warm Springs, Georgia, Franklin Delano Roosevelt died from a cerebral hemorrhage, leaving a weary nation in shock.

Shortly after the president's death, his widow wrote, "He still held the fundamental feeling that religion was an anchor and a source of strength and guidance, so I am sure that he died looking into the future as calmly as he had looked at all the events of his life."

HIGHLIGHTS OF THE ADMINISTRATION OF FRANKLIN ROOSEVELT

- 1933—The Twentieth Amendment sets the term beginnings at January 3 for Congress and January 20 for the president and vice president.

- 1933—The Twenty-first Amendment repealed prohibition.

- 1933—Civilian Conservation Corps and Public Works Administration are established.

- 1933—Agricultural Adjustment Administration is established.

- 1933—Roosevelt begins his "fireside chats."

- 1933—Tennessee Valley Authority is established.

- 1935—Works Progress Administration is established.

- 1936—FDR is reelected to second term.

- 1940—FDR is reelected to unprecedented third term.

- 1941—America enters World War II following Japanese attack on Pearl Harbor.

- 1942—Roosevelt helps create the "Grand Alliance" against the Axis powers.

- 1944—FDR is reelected to fourth term.

- 1945—FDR dies from a massive stroke.

HARRY S TRUMAN (1884–1972)

State Born: Missouri   Occupation: Haberdasher

Party: Democrat   Religion: Baptist

HARRY S TRUMAN

THIRTY-THIRD PRESIDENT
1945–1953

At this moment, I have in my heart a prayer. I ask only to be a good and faithful servant of my Lord and my people.

—HARRY S TRUMAN,
*in his first speech to Congress,
shortly after becoming president*

He said "hell." He said "damn."

Both got him in trouble not only with some conservative Democrats and Republicans, but also with the Baptist Church, of which he was a member. Nevertheless, Harry S Truman was a tough-skinned, full-blooded pragmatist who knew what he wanted and, "if it made good sense," spoke his mind in spite of pending consequences.

A GENUINE PRAGMATIST

Harry Truman was not schooled in the sophisticated social graces displayed by his predecessor, and he definitely lacked the familiar "father image" that Americans had so long associated with FDR and others who were elected to the presidency. He refused to play politics for the sake of popular opinion. "I wonder how far Moses would have gone if he'd taken a poll in Egypt?" he asked. "What would Jesus Christ have preached if he'd taken a poll in Israel? Where would the Reformation had gone if Martin Luther had taken a poll? It isn't polls or public opinion at the moment that counts. It is right and wrong and leadership—men with fortitude, honesty, and a belief in the right that makes epochs in the history of the world."

Harry Truman didn't want to be president, but once catapulted into the Oval Office by President Roosevelt's death, the crusty former haberdasher from the plains of Missouri set out to get things done with a minimum amount of nonsense.

His critics said he was brash; his friends labeled him confident; syndicated columnist Max Lerner compared him to "a bantam cock in a bustling barnyard." By any interpretation, both friend and foe agreed that Truman spoke his mind in a staccato delivery that was a familiar trademark to reporters at press conferences. And there was no misunderstanding his rancor when he dashed off a stinging letter to the music critic who published a not-too-complimentary review of daughter Margaret's singing.

Truman's spontaneous evaluations were aimed at other people as well, including church members. Although, like Gandhi, the president loved his Lord, he sometimes found it difficult to love the Lord's followers. Truman was amazed, for example, that those who prayed for "peace on earth" on Sunday seemed to do everything possible to prevent it during the remainder of the week. "The quarrels between religions," he said, "cause many of our world's problems."

When certain groups claimed that "God is on *our* side," Truman countered, "People of *any* race, color, creed, or nation could be God's favorites—so long as they behave themselves."

This is not to say that Harry Truman was opposed to the organized church. To the contrary, the church had been a part of his life since childhood. In his *Memoirs*, he wrote that by the time he was fourteen years old, he had read his family Bible three times through. He even met his wife-to-be, Elizabeth ("Bess") Wallace, in a Baptist Sunday school in their hometown of Independence, Missouri. Young Harry was only six years old; Bess was five.

A Fight with His Pastor

President Truman was his own man, of that there can be no doubt. At the same time, he felt that, in the eyes of God, he was no better than anyone else.

He recorded in one of his diary entries that he liked to attend the First Baptist Church in Washington, because its minister, the Reverend Edward Hughes Pruden, treated him not as a celebrity but as any other member of the assembled congregation. By contrast, the pastor of another Washington church (unnamed in the diary) turned the occasion of his visits into a "show."

The president seemed quite at home in the First Baptist Church and on one occasion gave an impromptu address to the Sunday school children. But this association was soon to change.

In 1952, Truman was faced with a somewhat sticky situation. A strong ground swell of support emerged in Congress to send an ambassador to the Vatican in Rome. The president supported the idea and appointed his close friend, General Mark Clark, to the position. Truman knew that such a decision would surely get him in hot water, but by now he was used to the heat.

However, the Southern Baptist Convention could not stand idly by and let this happen, so at its annual assembly, the delegates chastised its most famous member for encouraging this proposal. Their protests bore striking resemblance to the warnings of possible Roman Catholic influence in American politics expressed during the Revolutionary period.

When he returned home from the convention, Reverend Pruden

met privately with President Truman in the White House behind closed doors for nearly an hour. As he was leaving, some reporters standing at the front gates asked the reason for his visit, to which Pruden replied, "I came to dissuade the president from sending an ambassador to the Vatican."

At breakfast the next morning, the president read the account of this conversation in the newspaper and slammed the paper to the table in disgust, knocking over a half-filled glass of orange juice. "Damn it!" he shouted. "This is a violation of confidence!" Harry Truman never again set foot in the First Baptist Church.

In a 1971 interview with Jerry Hess of the Truman Library, Reverend Pruden gave this account: "I did hear indirectly one or two little humorous remarks that [President Truman] made regarding the situation [the appointing of an ambassador to the Vatican]. Someone said they saw him at a flower show one Sunday morning, and when he left around ten-thirty, they said, 'Mr. President, are you going to church from here?' He said, 'No, my preacher and I have had a fight.' Later on, someone said they heard him comment on what a commotion some preachers had made about this Vatican appointment, and then he added, 'My preacher is the worst of all.'"

A MAN OF DECISIONS

When he felt he was right, President Truman was an impossible man to stop. He was in charge, made sure everyone knew it, and wasted little time in "taking matters under advisement." He made bold decisions, whether they involved dropping the first atomic bomb on Japanese soil or firing popular five-star general Douglas MacArthur for insubordination. He claimed he never lost one night's sleep over any decision once it was made.

Decisions were important to Harry Truman, especially decisions to make something happen for the better. He once told a friend, "We often hear it said that spiritual values are indestructible. But I think it should be said that they are indestructible only so long as men are ready and willing to take action to preserve them."

A Prayer to Do His Best

His first speech as president to a joint session of Congress contained a preview of coming attractions—a prophetic request mixed with religious overtones— "that I may discern between good and bad; for who is able to judge . . . so great a people? I only ask to be a good and faithful servant of my Lord and my people."

That rather lofty-sounding ideal notwithstanding, he repeated this thought in a manner that reflected more the Truman style when he told his daughter, Margaret, "Your dad will never be reckoned among the great. But you can be sure he did his level best and gave all he had to his country. There is an epitaph in Boot Hill Cemetery in Tombstone, Arizona, which reads, 'Here lies Jack Williams; he done his damnedest.' What more can a person do?"

His Favorite Prayer

That was classic Harry Truman. His quest to do the best with what the good Lord gave him underlined his entire life. The following note, in his own handwriting, was attached to Harry Truman's favorite prayer, which he kept on his White House desk. The president also carried a copy of it with him at all times.

This prayer has been said by me—Harry S Truman—from high school days, as a window washer, bottle duster, floor scrubber in an Independence, Missouri, drugstore, as a timekeeper on a railroad contract gang, as an employee of a newspaper, as a bank clerk, as a farmer riding a gangplow behind four horses and mules, as a fraternity official learning to say nothing at all if good could not be said of a man, as a public official judging the weaknesses and shortcomings of constituents, and as president of the United States of America."

O, almighty and everlasting God,
creator of heaven and earth and the universe:
Help me to be, to think, to act what
is right, because it is right.
Make me truthful, honest, and honorable
in all things.
Make me intellectually honest for the
sake of right and honor, and without thought
of reward to me.
Give me the ability to be charitable,
forgiving, and patient with my fellow men.
Help me to understand their motives and
their shortcomings—even as
Thou understandest mine.
Amen.

President Truman was a pragmatist not only in politics, but in theology as well. "The Sermon on the Mount," he said, "is the greatest of all things in the Bible, a way of life, and maybe someday men will get to understand it as the *real* way of life."

To Harry Truman, that just made good sense.

HIGHLIGHTS OF THE ADMINISTRATION OF HARRY TRUMAN

- 1945—World War II ends.

- 1945—United Nations is established.

- 1947—The Truman Doctrine and the Marshall Plan begin.

- 1948—Truman wins election to a full term.

- 1949—North Atlantic Treaty Organization (NATO) is established.

- 1950—U.S. military advisors are sent to Korea.

- 1951—The Twenty-second Amendment limits Presidents to two full terms in office.

- 1951—Truman removes General Douglas MacArthur from command.

- 1952—The first hydrogen bomb is exploded by the U.S. in the Pacific Ocean.

DWIGHT DAVID EISENHOWER (1890–1969)

State Born: Texas   Occupation: Soldier

Party: Republican   Religion: Presbyterian

DWIGHT DAVID
EISENHOWER

THIRTY-FOURTH PRESIDENT
1953–1961

Every gun that is made, every warship launched, every rocket fired signifies, in the final sense, a theft from those who hunger and are not fed, those who are cold and are not clothed. This world in arms is not about spending money alone. It is spending the sweat of its laborers, the genius of its scientists, the hopes of its children. . . . This is not a way of life at all, in any true sense. Under the cloud of threatening war, it is humanity hanging from a cross of iron.

—DWIGHT D. EISENHOWER

If there was nothing else in my life to prove the existence of an almighty and merciful God, the events of the next twenty-four hours did it. This is what I found out about religion: It gives you courage to make the decisions you must make in a crisis, and then the confidence to leave the results to a higher power. Only by trust in oneself and trust in God can a man carrying responsibility find repose."

With these words, General Dwight David Eisenhower recalled his anxiety over the postponement of D-Day in June 1944. He maintained this personal theology when he served as the thirty-fourth president of the United States.

Dwight David Eisenhower

INAUGURATION PRAYER

Before his inauguration in 1953, the former supreme commander of Allied armies in Europe during World War II, his family, along with members of his cabinet and their families, quietly went to the National Presbyterian Church in Washington for prayer and meditation. Following the service, the elected president, in a sweeping victory over Democratic rival Adlai Stevenson composed a prayer. It read, in part:

> Almighty God, as we stand here at this moment, my future associates in the executive branch of government join me in beseeching that thou will make full and complete our dedication to the service of the people in this throng, and their fellow citizens everywhere. Give us, we pray, the power to discern right from wrong, and allow all our words and actions to be governed thereby, and by the laws of our land.

With this prayer, on January 20, 1953, Eisenhower began his inaugural address.

While other presidents referred to Almighty God at the conclusion of their first official speeches to the American public—as if this was an appropriate way to sign off—Dwight Eisenhower was the only one who boldly *began* his first inaugural address with a prayer.

Prayer had always been a part of President Eisenhower's Christian heritage. At the same time, some of the other so-called normal activities associated with the faith were missing.

ADULT BAPTISM

The Eisenhower family in Abilene, Kansas, belonged to a sect known as the River Brethren, which frowned on infant baptism. Hence, young Ike learned to revere the Holy Scriptures, but he never got around to being baptized.

Not until after much prayerful consideration, on February 1, 1953, less than two weeks following his inauguration, did President Eisenhower kneel before the font at the National Presbyterian Church for the rite of Holy Baptism. "He has moved from one army post to another, and has never staked down his faith," said officiating clergyman, Dr. Edward L. R. Elson, immediately following the private ceremony in the church.

DEVOTIONS WHILE PRESIDENT

During his administration, President Eisenhower began several traditions that had a religious emphasis, including a practice of beginning each meeting of the cabinet with a silent prayer and also hosting the first presidential prayer breakfast at Washington's Mayflower Hotel. The tradition became so popular that overflow crowds dictated moving the breakfast to the more spacious Hilton Hotel, where the breakfasts are held to this day.

On Sunday mornings, the president would be seen entering the National Presbyterian Church. When on several occasions he returned to the White House from an extended trip abroad, and it happened to be on a Sunday morning, he would step from the helicopter, speak a few words to the press, go inside to change clothes, and immediately head for church services.

However, as all presidents were quick to realize, there was little he could do without becoming subjected to criticism. President Eisenhower's practice of attending church drew comments from Senator Matthew Neeley (Democrat, West Virginia) who charged that the president's public worship smacked of hypocrisy. He felt that if the president wanted to pray, he should "shut the door and pray in secret." Neither President nor Mrs. Eisenhower responded to the senator's charge.

A BASIC APPROACH TO THE FAITH

Upon leaving the White House after two four-year full terms, the former president and his wife, Mamie, became members of the Presbyterian Church of Gettysburg, Pennsylvania, on February 1, 1961 (the anniversary of his baptism). His new pastor, the Reverend Robert A. MacAskill, recalled, "The Eisenhowers set a good example by their regular attendance at worship, and they made the rest of us feel better just by being there."

Reverend MacAskill points to the fact that President Eisenhower endorsed a strong concept of "a sovereign God who ruled all nations and peoples."

MacAskill, who was undoubtedly closer to this president than was any other clergyman, summarized Eisenhower's basic approach to his faith: "If each of us in his own mind would dwell upon the simple virtues—integrity, courage, self-confidence, and unshakable belief in his Bible—would not some of our problems tend to simplify themselves?"

That was straightforward and to the point. That was Dwight David Eisenhower.

HIGHLIGHTS OF THE ADMINISTRATION OF DWIGHT DAVID EISENHOWER

- 1953—Truce with Korea is signed.

- 1955—Eisenhower survives a heart attack.

- 1956—The Salk polio vaccine was put on the market.

- 1956—Eisenhower is reelected to a second term in office.

- 1956—Eisenhower establishes the Interstate Highway Act.

- 1957—Eisenhower sends federal troops to Little Rock, Arkansas, to ensure integration of schools.

- 1959—Alaska and Hawaii become states.

JOHN FITZGERALD KENNEDY (1917–1963)

State Born: Massachusetts   Occupation: Politician

Party: Democrat   Religion: Roman Catholic

JOHN FITZGERALD KENNEDY

THIRTY-FIFTH PRESIDENT
1961–1963

I am not the Catholic candidate for president. I am the Democratic Party's candidate for president who happens to be a Catholic.

—JOHN F. KENNEDY,
1960 campaign speech

He had all the credentials of a superb presidential candidate. He came from a solid New England family. He was wealthy, handsome, articulate, educated, brilliant, energetic, and clever. Only one thing stood in his way: he was a Roman Catholic.

During the early days of the campaign of 1960, John Fitzgerald Kennedy's Roman Catholic faith caused even some of the staunchest Democrats to fear that, if elected, his policies (and those of the nation) would be dictated by the Vatican. Others feared that his Catholic heritage would hurt any chance of gaining election as it did for candidate Alfred E. Smith in 1928.

MEETING THE CATHOLIC ISSUE HEAD ON

Pockets of fundamentalism coupled with anti-Catholic prejudice still existed in the nation, particularly in the so-called Bible Belt states—North and South Carolina, Tennessee, Kentucky, Georgia, Florida, Mississippi, Alabama, Arkansas, and Texas. Many Protestants feared that, were Kennedy elected as president, our national policies would be shaped not in Washington but in Rome. They were concerned that as president, Kennedy would be compelled to follow the dictates of the pope.

In typical style, the young Massachusetts Democrat met the issue head-on, and he left no doubt as to where he stood on the subject of church and state, particularly as it related to the presidency. Just eight months before the election in 1960, Kennedy spelled out his philosophy in a *Look* magazine article. "Whatever one's religion in his private life may be for the office-holder nothing takes precedence over his oath to uphold the Constitution and all of its parts—including the First Amendment and the strict separation of church and state."

One month later he told a group of newspaper editors, "I am not the Catholic candidate for president. I do not speak for the Catholic Church on issues of public policy, and no one in that church speaks for me."

Perhaps he was most convincing when he gave a dramatic speech in September before a gathering of Protestant ministers in Houston, Texas. There he displayed the famous Kennedy ability to turn adversity into an advantage when he told them, "Because I am a Catholic, and no Catholic has been elected president, it is apparently necessary for me to state once again . . . not what kind of church I believe in for that should be important only to me, but what kind of America I believe in. I believe in an America where separation of church and state is absolute, where no Catholic prelate would tell the president (should he be Catholic) how to act, and no Protestant minister would tell his parishioners for whom to vote."

THE KENNEDY ADVANTAGES

Aside from his remarkable ability to win over even his strongest critics, Kennedy had three other advantages over former Catholic candidate Al Smith. First, the spirit of peaceful coexistence perpetuated by former President Eisenhower did much to ease tensions between Roman Catholics and Protestants. Second, the Catholic Church made a conscientious effort to downplay its familiar claim as being the "only true Church." Finally, the presence of Pope John XXIII in the Vatican was of great comfort to both Catholics and non-Catholics. This fatherly figure who radiated love and concern for all God's children quickly dispelled any notion that Rome was a threat to the security of the United States.

John XXIII was a new breed of pope; John F. Kennedy represented the modern version of Catholicism.

John Kennedy won the election in 1960, but it was not easy. He squeezed past the Republican nominee, Richard Nixon, by less than 113,000 votes. Some analysts felt that Kennedy's religion actually helped him as much as it hurt him in the election. Nevertheless, it was the president's conduct that did the most to keep the matter stilled during his 1,036 days in office.

Although he was a faithful attender of mass, the president was reluctant to invite Roman Catholic priests to the Executive Mansion for fear of misinterpretation by the press and other observers. Also, during his administration, he showed no religious favoritism in his selection of staff members; he recommended no ambassador to the Vatican (something which even Harry Truman, a Baptist, had seriously considered); he did not hinder legislation regarding birth control; and, on occasion, he attended special services at Protestant churches.

A PROBLEM AT CONFESSION

As was the case with most chief executives, President Kennedy remained cautious about confiding in others, even to clergymen. He often worried that a visit to the confession booth (a standard procedure for faithful Catholics) would prove disastrous were some priest to recognize his voice and reveal the contents of his confession. In order to avoid recognition as much as possible, the president attended confession along with a group of Roman Catholic Secret Service agents, and he waited his turn in line with other parishioners.

In the popular compendium, *The People's Almanac,* Michael Medved relates that once, when the president entered the booth, his familiar voice was recognized by the priest.

"Good evening, Mr. President," said the priest.

"Good evening, Father," answered Kennedy, who then quickly arose and walked out.

HIS SPIRITUAL COUNSELORS

In spite of this, President Kennedy counted among his friends, two priests in whom he placed his trust. One was Richard Cardinal Cushing of Boston. An old friend of the Kennedy clan, Cushing officiated at Kennedy's marriage to socially prominent Jacqueline Bouvier in 1953 and baptized their children.

JFK's other confidant was his "pastor in Washington," Father Albert Pereira of St. Stephen's Church in Middleburg, Virginia, located near a country home purchased by President and Mrs. Kennedy in 1961. The president would often arrive a few minutes before Mass in order to chat privately with Father Pereira and according to the priest, displayed a remarkable awareness of the finer points of Catholic dogma.

Former U.S. Senate chaplain Edward Elson agreed with Father Pereira. "President Kennedy found it easy to talk about his religious convictions," he said. "At the same time, he was highly aware of the necessity to keep religion and matters of state separate."

THE KENNEDY MYSTIQUE

John Kennedy had an uncanny ability to sway crowds. His youth, charm, and polish created a vibrant charisma, not only in America but in other lands as well.

In 1961, during a visit to France at a time when fashion-minded designers copied his wife's stylish clothes and hairdos, the president introduced himself as "the man who accompanied Jacqueline Kennedy to Paris."

Later that year, he stood alongside the Berlin Wall which separated family and friends of West Germany and East Germany. He captured the hearts of the people, drawing cheers from an assembled throng, as he proclaimed his empathy by shouting, *"Ich bin ein Berliner!"*

Perhaps his personal ethos was never more evident than at the time he returned to the soil of his ancestors in the spring of 1963 and spoke to the people of Ireland about his heritage. "When my great-grandfather left here, he carried with him two things—a strong religious faith and a strong desire for liberty. I am glad to say that all of his great-grandchildren valued that inheritance."

PRAYER IN PUBLIC SCHOOLS

During President Kennedy's term in office, he and Congress had to wrestle with a controversial decision regarding prayer in public schools.

Prior to June 17, 1963, most school days began with a teacher reading ten verses from the Bible without offering comment, The students, then, prayed aloud the Lord's Prayer.

If parents objected to this practice, all they had to do was write a note explaining their feelings. Their children would thereby be excused from participation in this ritual.

The Supreme Court ruled on June 17 that this mandatory practice was to cease. The Court cited the First Amendment of the Constitution as the basis for this decision.

Because of his Roman Catholic faith, President Kennedy was falsely accused by some of his political foes for encouraging this decision.

Assassination

On Friday, November 22, 1963, at 12:30 p.m. in Dallas, Texas, a sniper's bullet killed the president of the United States, and weeping America said good-bye to its thirty-fifth chief executive.

HIGHLIGHTS OF THE ADMINISTRATION OF JOHN FITZGERALD KENNEDY

- 1961—JFK establishes the Peace Corps.

- 1961—The ill-fated "Bay of Pigs" invasion takes place.

- 1962—JFK imposes a quarantine on Cuba during the Missile Crisis.

- 1963—President Kennedy is assassinated in Dallas, Texas.

LYNDON BAINES JOHNSON (1908–1973)

State Born: Texas

Party: Democrat

Occupation:
Teacher/Politician

Religion: Disciples of
Christ

LYNDON BAINES JOHNSON

THIRTY-SIXTH PRESIDENT

1963–1969

No man could live in the house where I live and work at the desk where I work, without needing and seeking the support of earnest and frequent prayer. Prayer has helped me bear the burdens of the first office, which are too great to be borne by anyone alone.

—LYNDON B. JOHNSON

Lyndon Baines Johnson was a crowd pleaser. Nothing delighted him more than to win the admiration of the multitudes. To the dismay of Secret Service agents, our thirty-sixth president often slipped out of their protective ring just to shake hands with people along a parade route or, without warning, took a break from the routine of the Oval Office and walked outside to talk with visitors standing in line awaiting a tour of the White House. Lyndon Johnson loved their attention and behaved much like an actor who lives on applause.

Lyndon Baines Johnson

An Ecumenical President

Johnson was attracted to several different communions within the Christian church. His mother was a Baptist, and he married Lady Bird, a strong Episcopalian. The president, from his youth, was a member of the Disciples of Christ.

Because of this diverse background and his desire to please everybody, it should come as no surprise that President Johnson attended more Washington churches—both Protestant and Catholic—than any other president. Even on the day of his inauguration in 1965, he played both sides of the ecumenical fence. At nine o'clock in the morning, along with Vice President Hubert H. Humphrey and other national leaders, President Johnson attended an interfaith religious service at the National City Christian Church at which a Catholic priest, a Protestant minister, and a rabbi offered prayers.

Attending church service was not always a retreat from his problems, for on November 12, 1967, while worshiping at historic Bruton Parish Church in Williamsburg, Virginia, the president was publicly chastised from the pulpit for his policies on Vietnam. Upon leaving the service, his wife, Lady Bird, fuming inside but keeping her composure, let it be known to Reverend Cotesworth Pinckney Lewis how she felt about his sermon. "The choir anthem was lovely," she said.

Religious Advisers

For reasons known only to himself, President Johnson surrounded himself with advisers having strong church ties. Two of the more prominent were Press Secretary Bill Moyers, an ordained Baptist minister, and evangelist Billy Graham, a frequent visitor to the White House, who was labeled by the press as a "member of the Cabinet, ex officio."

Brother Fabian, a priest at St. Dominic's Roman Catholic

Church in Washington, D.C., had gained the respect and trust of the president, who enjoyed sitting inside the sanctuary to meditate. Brother Fabian, in fact, even gave President Johnson a key to the church so he could come and go even during the early hours of the morning.

Today, at St. Dominic's, a plaque on a one of its pillars reminds visitors of the numerous visits made to the parish by President Johnson.

IMPORTANCE OF PRAYER

President Johnson worked hard, played hard, and prayed hard. He said, "No man could live in the house where I live, and work at the desk where I work, without needing and seeking the support of earnest and frequent prayer. Prayer has helped me to bear the burdens of the first office, which are too great to be borne by anyone alone."

These burdens to which he referred were suddenly thrust upon him by the sniper's bullet that killed President John F. Kennedy on the afternoon of November 22, 1963. The entire world ground to a halt and watched as the tragic events unfolded, including a video replay of the shooting . . . a rush of cars to the hospital . . . a blood-stained pink suit . . . a bronze coffin . . . and a tall Texan aboard *Air Force One* with his left hand on President Kennedy's personal Bible, haltingly raising his right hand to take the oath of office from Justice Sarah Hughes. Lyndon Baines Johnson became the president of a nation in mourning.

At one minute before six, Washington time, *Air Force One* landed at Andrews Air Force Base. It was dark. Only after the body of the fallen president, accompanied by Mrs. Kennedy, was removed from the plane did the newly sworn president appear. He was drawn, tired, disheveled, and bent over like a man twice his age. He approached a microphone, reached into his coat pocket, drew out a piece of paper, and delivered the shortest inaugural address in the nation's history: "This is a sad time for all people. We have suffered a great loss that cannot be weighed. For me, it is a deep personal tragedy. I know the world shares the sorrow that Mrs. Kennedy and her family bear. I will do my best. That is all I can do. I ask for your help—and God's."

HIS OUTSPOKEN COMMITMENT

Lyndon Johnson didn't like funerals, and he wasn't going to let the effects of this one linger any longer than necessary. He was a man who enjoyed getting things done. With his political savvy, he played Congress like a master musician would his violin. He had relentless drive, and if fighting and arm-twisting were necessary, so be it.

One of the driving forces behind the new president was his obsession with a dream for a better America—a compassionate, loving, and caring America. He fought for what he called the Great Society, where every person—rich or poor, black or white—could prosper.

Lyndon Johnson treated this compelling drive to serve humanity as though it were a mandate from God. At a presidential prayer breakfast on February 1, 1961, then Vice President Johnson had said, "We need to remember that the separation of church and state must never mean the separation of religious values from the lives of public servants. If we who serve free men today are to differ from the tyrants of this age, we must balance the powers in our hands with God in our hearts."

Later, that same year, at a Christmas pageant for peace, Johnson boldly proclaimed, "Let no one mistake the American purpose. Our nation is dedicated to Christ's quest for peace—not the false peace of evasion and retreat, but the divine peace which comes as the fulfillment of striving and the climax of commitment. We shall never falter in that dedication."

These weren't just his goals; the president insisted that the author of such a society was Almighty God. He once suggested that a monument be built in the capital, a city full of monuments, in honor of God. This idea never got beyond the planning stage, and to the astonishment of the president, it was the conservative church leaders who rebelled. In their opinion, such a monument might imply support of the claim by radical theologians that "God is dead."

Lyndon B. Johnson shook his head in utter disbelief. This interpretation was impossible for someone who was such a great believer in himself, in his nation, and in his God.

HIGHLIGHTS OF THE ADMINISTRATION OF LYNDON BAINES JOHNSON

- 1964—Johnson signs into law the Civil Rights Act.

- 1964—Johnson is elected to his first full term in office.

- 1964—The Gemini space program begins.

- 1965—The Medicare Act provides medical care for older citizens under the Social Security system.

- 1965—First U.S. troops are sent to Vietnam.

- 1965—The Twenty-fifth Amendment states that the vice president, in the event of the death or resignation of the chief executive, becomes president.

- 1968—Johnson announces that he will not seek reelection.

RICHARD MILHOUS NIXON (1913–1994)

State Born: California   Occupation: Lawyer

Party: Republican   Religion: Society of Friends (Quaker)

RICHARD MILHOUS
NIXON

THIRTY-SEVENTH PRESIDENT

1969–1974

Mr. Nixon would have profited by a pastor. Billy Graham, who frequented the White House, is an evangelist; this is a different breed from a pastor. Every man in the world has the right to have a spiritual confidant to whom he can say anything and from whom he can hear anything.

—DR. EDWARD L. R. ELSON,
former U.S. Senate chaplain, 1978

When the history books are written," said an Associated Press release of August 9, 1974 (the day Nixon resigned from office), "the presidency of Richard Milhous Nixon will be placed in its proper perspective."

Most people find it difficult to be objective about him. Visitors to Tussaud's Wax Museum in London answered questionnaires which asked, "What person do you most hate and fear?" Topping the list in 1974 was Richard Nixon. Today, some observers in America and throughout the world regard him as a martyr, even a folk hero.

A Career Overflowing with Controversy

Both the man and his political career were marked with personal triumphs and rocked by bitter defeats. Friends he trusted betrayed him, and confidential communications were leaked to the press. Stories were blown out of proportion.

The former vice president under Dwight Eisenhower lost the presidential election of 1960 and the race for governor of California in 1962. The defeats hurt him deeply—especially the one in '62, after which Nixon vowed never again to enter the arena of politics.

Yet after a time for healing, he again thrust himself into the spotlight and pushed forward against incredible odds. He regained his national popularity and won the election for president in 1968 by a plurality; in 1972, he won reelection by the largest majority of any presidential candidate in history until that time.

Because of his unwavering self-determination and inner conviction, it is difficult to pigeonhole Richard Nixon in terms of his principles—including his religious beliefs.

Quaker Upbringing

When Nixon was nine years old, his parents moved to Whittier, California, then a small Quaker community, and that is the closest connection the thirty-seventh president had with the Society of Friends. His youth, he said, consisted of "family, church, and school." But as he grew older, he parted ways with his fellow Quakers.

Unlike Herbert Hoover (the only other Quaker president), Nixon never attended the Friends' meeting house while living in Washington, D.C. Instead, he seemed quite comfortable with a variety of other communions, choosing to attend different churches without identifying with any one of them.

The now-famous tapes of White House conversations in the

Oval Office during the Nixon administration (made public during the Watergate hearings) revealed that the president's actions were guided by a passion for maintaining the sovereignty of his office coupled with bitter memories of those former confidants who he felt had betrayed him. This could explain why Nixon kept himself at arm's length from both individuals and organizations and perhaps why he became so religiously insulated against the organized Church.

INFLUENCE OF BILLY GRAHAM

The spiritual adviser closest to the president was evangelist Billy Graham. According to former speechwriter Pat Buchanan, the entire White House staff once went en masse to a Billy Graham crusade in Pittsburgh. "It was the president's idea," said Buchanan.

Billy Graham was a favorite of President Nixon. According to Dr. Edward L. R. Elson, former chaplain of the United States Senate, "Nixon would have profited by a pastor. Billy Graham . . . is an evangelist; this is a different breed from a pastor. Every man in this world has the right to have a spiritual confidant to whom he can say anything and from whom he can hear anything."

Chaplain Elson's comments invite debate. Nonetheless, it was an experience of President Nixon's at one of Billy Graham's crusades that may have been one of the reasons that the president shunned public worship. After just sixteen months in office, the president appeared as a guest at one of the Graham crusades. As he attempted to speak from the platform, Nixon was heckled by antiwar protesters in the audience.

The president's closest association with a church and congregational life was in Key Biscayne, Florida, where he spent many days during his administration relaxing and enjoying life with his friend, Bebe Rebozo. The Reverend John Huffman, pastor of Key Biscayne

Presbyterian Church, relates that the president was a frequent visitor to services. On the day the Vietnam War finally ended, the president requested a special service of prayer to be held at the church that evening.

Outside of that, Nixon seldom attended public worship. Instead, he devised a new plan.

Chapel in the White House

Shortly after his inauguration in 1969, President Nixon invited prominent clergymen throughout the country to come to the Executive Mansion on Sunday mornings to lead an assembled body of three hundred to four hundred people—also invited by the president—in worship in the East Room. Charles "Bud" Wilkerson, former Oklahoma University football coach, made the arrangements and carefully outlined the protocol for the invited clergymen, which included the admonition to limit the sermon to fifteen minutes, because "the president doesn't like long messages."

This unique arrangement often proved frustrating to the designated minister. Due to the president's erratic schedule, sometimes a call went out as late as Friday to a minister who was asked to rearrange his schedule, pack his suitcase, and be in Washington before ten o'clock on Sunday morning.

If this mode of worship didn't shatter precedent, it bent it out of recognizable shape. Like the rest of us mortals, even a chief executive who attempts to alter tradition is vulnerable to public rebuke. In a June 1969 edition of the *Washington Daily News* President Nixon's style of worship was criticized as a "Madison Avenue gimmick."

"Who does he think he is? Why doesn't he attend church like everyone else?" some asked.

Reinhold Niebuhr, prominent American theologian, was even stronger in his criticism. "President Nixon has turned the East Room into a kind of sanctuary and, by a curious combination of innocence and guile, has circumvented the Bill of Rights' first article."

The president explained his intramural approach to worship this way: "I could not as president attend a regular church service without being a source of distraction to the congregation and the cause of all manner of special preparation." However, his explanation fell upon deaf ears, and after two short years, this practice quietly faded away.

One psychologist was reported in a national news story that he felt President Nixon's "chapel in the White House" approach to worship was akin to the lifestyle of a European king who lived in a castle with its own chapel. "It shows that this man really sought to be a king rather than a president," said the psychologist.

That remark brought back memories of the time the president attempted to dress White House guards in white military uniforms fashioned by a European designer. This, too, resembled the atmosphere surrounding a monarchy.

MORE SETBACKS

These reactions were only foretastes of the future. As so often happened during his term of office, when President Nixon attempted to do what he thought was right, he suffered a setback in the eyes of many Americans.

Setbacks were certainly nothing new to this president. Moving to New York to practice law following his defeat for the governorship of California in '62, Nixon was a forgotten man. Most considered him a political lightweight. Even those close to him kept him at arm's length. Everyone, that is, except one—fellow attorney John Mitchell. Their friendship had deepened during those lonely years during which Nixon inched his way back up the political ladder.

After what the Associated Press labeled the "greatest comeback of all time" in the presidential victory of 1968, Nixon appointed his dear friend, John Mitchell, as attorney general.

Watergate and Resignation

On June 17, 1972, five men were apprehended while burglarizing the Democratic National Committee's headquarters in the Watergate Hotel. John Mitchell told the president that he (Mitchell) was involved. The president, out of loyalty, tried to protect his trusted friend through a cover-up that failed miserably. Taped conversations, congressional investigations, sworn testimony by eyewitnesses, and public outcries sealed his fate.

Senator Barry Goldwater, perhaps the most respected Republican on Capitol Hill, called upon President Nixon to resign. Goldwater, noted for his bluntness in telling the truth, informed the president that impeachment loomed on the horizon and that Nixon could count on only four or five of the Senate to support him.

The Oval Office of the White House is said to be the loneliest room in the world. When occupied by a rugged individualist so dedicated to the protection of this office, its demands eventually were bound to bring the president to his knees, especially in the wake of such a major trauma.

On August 7, 1974, as Nixon met in the Lincoln Sitting Room with Secretary of State Henry Kissinger, a Jew, he revealed his plan. Together the former Quaker and the Jew knelt for prayer—hard prayer.

Two days later, facing the possibility of impeachment charges, Richard Nixon went on television and resigned as president of the United States "for the sake of the office," the only president to do so.

Before he died on April 22, 1994, President Nixon regained praise, even from some of his former enemies, as an elder statesman, and he left a sage piece of advice in his parting words to America:

"Always remember others may hate you, but those who hate you don't win unless you hate them. And then you destroy yourself."

HIGHLIGHTS OF THE ADMINISTRATION OF RICHARD MILHOUS NIXON

- 1969—America makes first landing on the moon.
- 1971—The Twenty-sixth Amendment of the Constitution lowers the voting age to eighteen.
- 1972—President Nixon reduces tensions with China through a personal visit.
- 1972—Break-in takes place at the Democratic Headquarters at the Watergate Hotel in Washington.
- 1972—Nixon is elected to a second term in office.
- 1973—Cease-fire announced in Vietnam.
- 1974—President Nixon resigns from office.

GERALD RUDOLPH FORD (1913–)

State Born: Nebraska   Occupation: Lawyer

Party: Republican   Religion: Episcopalian

GERALD RUDOLPH FORD

THIRTY-EIGHTH PRESIDENT

1974–1977

*He was genuine beyond reproach, a "working-Episcopalian" who wasn't
ashamed to put his faith into practice.*

—Dr. Edward L. R. Elison,
former U. S. Senate chaplain, about Gerald Ford

M r. Vice President," intoned Chief Justice Warren Burger, "are you
prepared to take the oath of office as president of the United States?"

"I am, responded the strapping, six-foot-tall, former football player
from the University of Michigan.

As the country was reeling over the confusion of the past few days,
sharing their anxiety was the man who was about to grasp the reins of
responsibility left dangling by another. For the first time in history, a
president had resigned as America's chief executive.

Less than thirteen hours earlier, President Richard M. Nixon told
a national television audience, "In turning over direction of the
government to Vice President Ford, I know, as I told the nation
when I nominated him for that office ten months ago [to replace

Spiro T. Agnew, who had resigned], that the leadership of America will be in good hands."

At noon, Eastern Daylight Time, on August 9, 1974, in the East Room of the White House, packed with reporters, friends, and government officials, and with his wife, Betty, at his side, Vice President Gerald R. Ford raised his right hand and placed his left on a Bible opened to Proverbs 3:5–6, which read, "Trust in the LORD with all thine heart; and lean not unto thine own understanding. In all thy ways acknowledge him, and he shall direct thy paths."

It was Mr. Ford's favorite passage of Holy Scripture, one which he repeated every night as a prayer.

The brief inaugural address that followed held more religious overtones: "As we bind up the internal wounds of Watergate, let us restore the Golden Rule to our political process, and let brotherly love purge our hearts of suspicion and hate."

For Gerald Ford, religious observance was not for official ceremonies only, but it remained an important dimension of his life.

EARLY RELIGIOUS TRAINING

His mother and stepfather, whose name he had been given (his mother divorced his biological father when he was an infant) were staunch Episcopalians in Grand Rapids, Michigan. Gerald Ford and his bride, Betty, were married there in Grace Episcopal Church. When they moved to Washington, Betty taught Sunday school at Immanuel Church; young Gerald was active in men's clubs.

His religious observances took on other dimensions. For example, he was a regular attender of weekly congressional prayer breakfasts. He also befriended a feisty Michigan clergyman, the Reverend Billy Zeoli, president of Gospel Films. Zeoli, who often conducted chapel services for the Detroit Tigers baseball club, carried a positive enthusiasm about the message of Christianity— one that Gerald Ford welcomed, especially during the turbulent

1960s, when many in the nation were bent on striking out at all organizations, including the church.

On December 6, 1973, immediately after becoming vice president, Gerald Ford visited the Prayer Room of the Capitol for private meditation. It was in this same room that he, while vice president, and even after assuming the duties of president, along with four regulars (Representative John Rhodes of Arizona, Representative Charles Goodell of New York, former secretary of defense Melvin Laird of Wisconsin, and Representative Albert Quie of Minnesota), met at noon for fifteen minutes every Wednesday. Together, they prayed for the blessings of God upon this nation and upon themselves.

"Gerald Ford had no parade of piety," said former chaplain of the Senate Edward Elson. "He was genuine beyond reproach, a 'working Episcopalian' who wasn't ashamed to put his faith into practice."

Public worship was not uncommon for both Congressman and Mrs. Ford. Along with friends and neighbors they had gotten to know during their twenty-eight years in Washington, they had joined Immanuel Church on the Hill in Alexandria, Virginia, where their children were baptized. During Ford's brief term as president, he and Betty attended St. John's Episcopal Church in Lafayette Square for Sunday morning services.

"At times," said the Reverend Peter M. Larsen, assistant pastor of St. John's, "Mr. Ford would slip into the eight o'clock morning worship almost unnoticed by the twenty or thirty others present."

Chaplain Elson observed, "President Gerald Ford was unassuming and genuinely honest in his politics. He once said to me, 'You have to give a little, take a little, to get what you really want. But you don't have to give up your principles.'"

A MAN OF PRINCIPLE

His principles, according to some analysts, led to his defeat in the 1976 election. Just one month following his inauguration, Ford granted former president Nixon a "full, complete, and absolute pardon" for all federal crimes which he might have committed as chief executive.

It was a rough decision that, according to President Ford, he did not treat lightly. On the day he made that decision, he attended St. John's Episcopal Church across the street from the White House to pray for guidance and understanding. He received Holy Communion, then returned to the Oval Office, where he finalized the statement with the announcement that would leave a powerful impact upon his future.

The grumbling never ceased after that Sunday morning. Potential supporters fell away, and the pardon became a major campaign issue for the Democrats and their front-runner, Jimmy Carter, who won the election in 1976.

Although he acknowledged that his pardoning Nixon was not in his best interests politically, Gerald Ford did not regret his decision. "I only did what I thought was right," he said.

HIGHLIGHTS OF THE ADMINISTRATION OF GERALD RUDOLPH FORD

- 1974—Ford issues a full pardon to former President Nixon.

- 1974—Trade Reform Act gives the president power to negotiate or withhold foreign trade agreements.

- 1975—American involvement in Vietnam ends.

- 1976—President Ford loses his bid for reelection to Governor Jimmy Carter.

JAMES EARL CARTER (1913–)

State Born: Georgia   Occupation: Farmer/Naval Officer

Party: Democrat   Religion: Baptist

JAMES EARL
CARTER

THIRTY-NINTH PRESIDENT

1977–1981

*Washington, D.C. is now the only city in the world where someone can call
"Dial-a-prayer" and get the White House.*

—BOB HOPE, *Comedian*

For Jimmy Carter, the church is an important part of his life. My
husband would be lost without it," said Rosalynn Carter on
WROD's radio talk show in Daytona Beach, Florida, during his
successful presidential campaign in 1975. President James Earl
"Jimmy" Carter represented a type of religious conviction unknown
by former tenants of the White House. Unlike many of his predecessors, whose associations with the organized church were aloof
and little more than academic, President Carter (given the code
name "Deacon" by the Secret Service) immersed himself in his
beliefs.

A Born-Again Christian

As a Southern Baptist and born-again Christian, Carter is never reluctant to confess, "I am a Christian," or to take the opportunity to say, "Let me tell you what Christ means to me."

"This fundamentalistic, 'Brother, are you saved?' piety and zeal was the sort of thing one expected to find on Sunday mornings on little southern radio stations," wrote James Wooten, White House correspondent for the *New York Times,* "but not from a man seeking such an office as he."

Strangely, it worked for Jimmy Carter. In spite of the fact he proclaimed his faith without apology, Carter slowly climbed the ladder of success in political circles that were accustomed neither to his attitude nor to the uniquely Christian phrases he sprinkled throughout his public speeches.

He taught the adult Sunday school class in his hometown congregation in Plains, Georgia. And while serving as Georgia governor and as president of the United States, he delighted in the chance to witness for his faith.

A Controversial Interview

Once, he may have carried his missionary zeal a bit too far—even in the eyes of his fellow conservative Baptists. During the campaign of 1975–76, Carter consented to an interview to be printed in the sexually oriented *Playboy* magazine. When challenged about appearing in this type of publication, Jimmy Carter responded, "Jesus commanded, 'Go into all the world and preach the gospel.' On this basis, I granted the interview."

The published interview nearly cost him the election. In it, Carter admitted that he sometimes entertained thoughts contrary to certain biblical admonitions—that sometimes he looked at a woman with "lust in his heart."

It was an honest observation for nearly any man, but it was one that Carter had to defend many times.

This innocent remark may have cost him some votes; nevertheless, Jimmy (as he preferred to be called) Carter defeated the incumbent, Gerald Ford, in a close election in 1976.

FINDING AN "ACCEPTABLE" SPIRITUAL HOME

One of the first orders of business for the Carter family was to search for a Baptist Church in Washington, D.C., as their new spiritual home. However even a personal decision such as this has political overtones. Which church should they select? It wasn't as easy a question to answer as it might first appear. There were other considerations and several alternatives. For instance, after an in-depth investigation by aides and advisers, the Carters realized they had to choose a church not only to their liking, but also one which would be "acceptable" to the people of the United States—one that maintained a Baptist flavor without giving the air of a camp meeting revival. In other words, the church would have to reflect a more "traditional" approach to worship.

Someone suggested that they attend a different church each Sunday—sort of a pinball approach—but the Carters wished to be active participants in a church, not just attenders.

Eventually, they selected the First Baptist Church pastored by the Reverend Charles Trentham, a minister who had an appreciation for liturgical worship while, at the same time, earning the reputation as a devoted Southern Baptist.

Even in the expression of religion through public worship, the office of the presidency is confining. Monday morning editions of newspapers throughout the nation often carried photos of the President and Mrs. Carter with captions of this nature: "President Carter is shown with a Bible tucked under his arm, leading his family to church for worship, where they sit in the sixth row of pews, right side, and together listen to Pastor Trentham—a man with whom the President has become close." Whenever possible, Mr. Carter picks up where he left off in Plains, Georgia, and conducts the adult Sunday school class.

Moral Imperatives

President Carter's first years in office were marked with a sharp focus on "moral imperatives." On both the national and the international scenes, he insisted on upholding the value of human rights. Syndicated columnist Jack Anderson observed, "Carter can see and smell the Atlanta ghetto where he once worked as a lay Baptist. . . . He can feel the impoverished Indian village where his mother labored as a Peace Corps volunteer. He identifies with those who need succor."

On the domestic scene, President Carter's close association with religion became the subject of criticism in some roundabout ways. When he urged widespread reform that might mean higher taxes for many citizens, one Republican congressman chided, "The trouble with Carter is he's listening only to God—and God doesn't pay taxes."

Although Jimmy Carter was a faithful member of the Southern Baptist denomination, he broke with its tradition when he openly supported civil rights. He made waves among many of his fellow parishioners when he sought racial equality for African-Americans. This was not something people expected—especially from a Southerner. But the president was convinced that he was doing the right thing. In a 1987 interview with author Richard Hutcheson, President Carter said, "The country at that time was searching for someone who would publicly profess a commitment to truth and integrity and the adherence to moral values—concerning peace, human rights, the alleviation of suffering—and I put forward these concepts which are very deeply ingrained in my own character and motivations."

As he served his four years as president, it was easy for the nation to see that the church meant more to President Carter than a place for a once-a-week visit.

Sophisticated theological works were part of his regular reading. Books by theologians Reinhold Niebuhr and Søren Kierkegaard—normally found on the shelves of clergymen and seminary students—were among his favorites. He quoted from them freely, even in his speeches to the American people. This caused some historians to label Carter as the most theologically literate president since Woodrow Wilson. At the same time, the president felt himself to be a student of theology rather than an expert.

FORSAKEN BY HIS BRETHREN

All the theology in the world was unable to ensure him longevity in office. The man who was elected to office amid the triumphant shouts of some conservative Christians that "one of us is in the White House," was soundly defeated in his bid for reelection, partly because of a well-organized and heavily financed campaign led by ultra-conservatives who felt the president had abandoned his principles. Many of the same faithful who applauded his victory in 1976 jumped ship and joined the ranks of his opponent, Ronald Wilson Reagan, in 1980, who they felt better served the cause of the Moral Majority, named and led by popular television evangelist Jerry Falwell.

OUR MOST IMPORTANT EX-PRESIDENT

The former president continues to work with a missionary enthusiasm, still convinced he can make a difference. A small black Bible is one of the few items on the desk in his office in the Carter Center, on a hilltop overlooking Atlanta. One week each year he and "Rosie" (a name he affectionately calls his wife) volunteer to work for Habitat for Humanity—a Christian-based group that builds low-cost houses that can be purchased by those who would otherwise never have an opportunity to own their own homes.

Whenever possible, Mr. Carter picks up where he left off in Plains, Georgia, before the fanfare that accompanies presidential campaigns and four years in the Oval Office. He conducts the adult Sunday school class at a local Baptist church.

How history will rate President Carter is yet unknown. However, we can be sure that his ability to influence Congress will not be noted as one of his strong points. Unlike predecessors such as Lyndon Johnson, who manipulated senators and legislators with ease, Jimmy Carter found dealing with Capitol Hill difficult, and his battles more often than not were futile.

As a Sunday school teacher and a lay leader within the Baptist Church, Jimmy Carter was reared in a society that believed, "Present the truth, and men will follow." But Congress isn't persuaded that way, and President Carter found it difficult to exchange the posture of a church leader for that of a political persuader.

What Rosalynn Carter said was true. For Jimmy Carter, the church is an important part of his life, perhaps even more important than the presidency itself.

HIGHLIGHTS OF THE ADMINISTRATION OF
JAMES EARL CARTER

- 1977—Carter signs the Panama Canal Treaty that gives control of the canal to the Panamanians by the year 2000.

- 1978—Helps create a peace treaty between Egypt and Israel through the Camp David Peace Accord, signed the next year.

- 1979—Carter signs the SALT II Treaty with Soviet Premier Leonid Brezhnev.

- 1979—The U.S. Department of Education is established.

- 1979—Iranians hold captive fifty-two Americans.

- 1980—Carter loses his bid for reelection to Governor Ronald W. Reagan.

RONALD WILSON REAGAN (1911–2004)

State Born: Illinois

Occupation: Actor/Public Official

Party: Republican

Religion: Disciples of Christ

RONALD WILSON
REAGAN

FORTIETH PRESIDENT
1981–1989

There are times when I'm in church I think God might recognize the magnitude of my responsibility and give me an extra portion of His grace. . . . and I don't feel guilty for feeling that way.

—RONALD REAGAN

He rode to office in one of the greatest landslides in political history, on the shoulders of a conservative wing of the Christian church known as the Moral Majority. Ronald Wilson Reagan, former film actor and governor of California, convinced the voting public that he, not Jimmy Carter, would be able to get the nation back on its feet—politically, economically, and spiritually.

FIRST INAUGURATION

In what could be described as one of the most patriotic days in American history, President Reagan's first inauguration in 1981 was but part of a bizarre set of events akin to the plot of a Hollywood B movie.

Those who attended the ceremony or who watched on television will remember seeing the beaming president-elect sitting beside a weary President Carter, whose face was drawn, almost void of emotion. To the podium stepped Reagan's confidant and friend, the Reverend Donn D. Moomaw, who echoed the drama of the moment in his inaugural prayer: "We thank you for the release of the hostages and for all those who made it possible. In this moment of new beginnings our hearts beat with a cadence of pride in our country and hope in its future."

For the last 444 days of the Carter Administration, fifty-two Americans were held captive in Iran as a result of the seizure of the American Embassy by alleged Iranian students. Despite diplomatic attempts to convince the Iranians to "let our people go," nothing happened. A bungled military attack backfired. Americans were growing increasingly impatient and embarrassed as veteran newsman Walter Cronkite ended each nightly broadcast reminding us just how many days up to that point the fifty-two had been in captivity.

Viewed by some as a final slap in the face of President Carter, Iran waited to free the hostages just hours before the new president took his oath of office on the west steps of the Capitol.

As the Mormon Tabernacle Choir sang "The Battle Hymn of the Republic" (President Reagan's favorite hymn) and bands paraded by, American flags seemed to fly a bit higher. Many observers felt a sense of renewed pride. They believed the new president had already established himself as a world leader who would make things happen. And happen they did.

The first few months of the Reagan administration were marked by cutbacks in domestic spending, elimination of several social programs, tax-cut proposals, and a bold effort to get the nation back on its feet through private enterprise. Ronald Reagan left no doubt in anyone's mind that he was in charge.

Part of that confidence lay in the president's firm belief that it was God who was in charge of him.

Calvinistic Roots

Shortly after being elected governor of California, he said, "I've always believed that there is a certain divine scheme of things. I'm not quite able to explain how my election happened or why I'm here, apart from believing that it's a part of God's plan for me." Later he added, "Faith in God is absolutely essential if a person is to do his best. Sometimes we're afraid to let people know that we rely on God. Taking this stand seems to be a logical and proper way to begin."

According to President Reagan, both man and God are partners in a synergistic approach to life. "There is nothing automatic about God's will," he said. "I think it is very plain that we are given a certain control of our destiny because we have a chance to choose. We are given a set of rules or guidelines in the Bible by which to live, and it is up to us to decide whether we will abide by them or not."

His mother, Nelle Wilson Reagan, encouraged him to read the Bible while growing up in Dixon, Illinois. Reagan's continual interest in the Bible and theology was due in part to the inspiration of the man to whom he referred throughout his terms in office as "my pastor," Donn Moomaw. Moomaw, a former UCLA football star, was pastor of Bel-Air Presbyterian Church in Los Angeles. Although the president was raised as a member of the Christian Church (Disciples of Christ), he had adopted this Presbyterian congregation as his own.

"It was love at first sight—or sound," explained Ronald Reagan. "We never listen to Donn that we don't feel richer for it. I can't recall when I've looked forward to going to church more. I guess my expectation comes from knowing I'll come away inspired."

In a letter dated February 25, 1981, Moomaw wrote about the most famous member of his flock: "I know the president as a man of faith in God. He is a man without guile and a very principled man."

REAGAN'S CHRISTIAN TESTIMONY

Unlike some of his predecessors, President Reagan never flinched from telling others about what and in whom he believed. One day he and evangelist Billy Graham discussed, in depth, the biblical prophecy concerning the second coming of Christ. According to those who heard the dialogue, Mr. Reagan held his own with the evangelist.

"After that conversation," said Reagan, "I asked Donn to send some more material on prophecies so I could check them out in the Bible for myself. You know, I was raised on the Bible. I also taught it for a long time in Sunday school."

Once when Christmas carolers serenaded then Governor Reagan in the rotunda of the State Capitol in Sacramento, California, he said to them, "My greetings are for those of all faiths, including those who believe Jesus was merely a great teacher and those who, like me, believe he is the promised Messiah, the Son of God."

Perhaps our most revealing insight into the president's faith centers in the "creed" he expressed several times:

> I believe that whatever has happened to me, whatever I've accomplished or attained, I could not have done without God's help. I believe that if I ever forget that part of my faith, if I ever forget what he has done or if I begin thinking I'm able to do something without his help, the blessings of faith will disappear as fast as an early snow. I simply believe that if you put your faith in God and ask for strength and wisdom to do what has to be done and at the same time do your best to do what you believe is right, you will be given the strength and wisdom to do it.

The president applied this creed to every dimension of his life. In a valentine he wrote in 1981 to Nancy, for example, he confessed he loved her "because you shared with me the belief that prayer and religion are private, but so vital and needed in all faiths and creeds at this time."

A Brush with Death

Perhaps the most revealing insight to President Reagan's faith came on March 30, 1981, when he was struck by a bullet fired by a would-be assassin.

Prior to going into surgery, the president told his physician, "I cannot ask God for help if I have hate in my heart for the one who shot me." He then uttered a prayer asking God's forgiveness for the man who pulled the trigger. The bullet missed the president's heart by only one inch.

Moomaw, who responded to a call from Nancy Reagan, was able to talk with the president later that evening.

"Ron," asked Moomaw, "if that bullet had taken you, would you have been okay with God?"

"Yes," answered the president without hesitation.

"How do you know?" asked Moomaw.

The president looked him squarely in the eye and said, "I have a Savior."

A few days later, according to his autobiography entitled *An American Life,* the president wrote in his diary: "Whatever happens now, I owe my life to God and will serve Him in every way I can." In this same spirit, he pledged to Terence Cardinal Cooke of New York: "Whatever time I have left is left for Him."

The attempt on President Reagan's life may have been a time for proclaiming his personal faith, yet without a doubt, it curtailed his habit of attending church. In 1984 a reporter asked him if he would attend church that next Sunday. The reporter quoted some critics who claimed that Ronald Reagan talked a lot about religion but wasn't seen at public worship.

The president admitted this was true. "I represent too much of a threat to too many other people for me to be able to go to church," he said. "And frankly, I miss it very much."

Much like the posture taken by Abraham Lincoln, who sat in the Oval Office more than one hundred years before him, Ronald Reagan did not unite solely with a particular congregation. Instead, his religion was more of a personal conviction based upon Christian teachings. But even more than Lincoln, President Reagan was willing to confess openly his belief in Jesus Christ as his Savior.

GOD'S PLAN FOR AMERICA

Donn Moomaw feels that Ronald Reagan's religious convictions were "more experiential than intellectual." That experience convinced Ronald Reagan that he had a mission of sorts, and that he, like the rest of us, had some part to play in God's plan. He wrote about this in a pointed letter to the mother of a handicapped boy:

> God has a plan for each one of us. Some with little faith and even less testing seem to miss in their mission, or else we perhaps fail to see their imprint on the lives of others. But bearing what we cannot change and going on with what God has given us, confident there is a destiny, somehow seems to bring a reward we wouldn't exchange for any other.

He even suggested that the nation and the church have a synergistic duty:

> We have it within our power to begin the world over again. We can do it, doing together what no one church can do by itself.

President Reagan served two terms in office. During this time he used his charm, wit and wisdom to win over his political enemies both at home and abroad. Representatives and senators on both sides of the aisle, while sometimes disagreeing with him on issues, found him to be likeable and a consummate gentleman.

The New Testament tells us that "the meek shall inherit the earth" (Psalm 37:11). If it is true that the term *meek* refers to "power with restraint," then President Ronald Reagan was the personification of that truth.

Before he left office, the president reminded the nation about their primary responsibility during his televised farewell remarks in January 1988. As he did during his Inaugural Address eight years earlier, he mentioned "the shining city on a hill"—a reference to the people of God described by Jesus during his Sermon on the Mount. It was a quote that the president used to project his view that America is the modern God-ordained beacon to the world of freedom and of hope.

A Long and Painful Farewell

In November 1994, President Reagan was diagnosed with Alzheimer's disease. During the next decade, Nancy devotedly comforted him as he steadily declined in health until he died, June 6, 2004.

At his burial site six days later at the Ronald Reagan Presidential Library in Simi Valley, California, his son, Ron, said that although his father never wore his faith on his sleeve to get votes, he believed that his primary responsibility was to serve the purpose of Almighty God.

Earlier that same morning, during the official State funeral for the 40th President, conducted at the National Cathedral in Washington, D.C., former Senator John Danforth, and Episcopal priest, officiated at the multi-faith service. In his homily, Danforth again read from the Sermon on the Mount, that included Reagan's favorite Biblical passage—"You are the light of the world. A city set on a hill cannot be hid."

Former Senator John Danforth then concluded, "If ever we have known a child of light, it was Ronald Reagan."

HIGHLIGHTS OF THE ADMINISTRATION OF
RONALD WILSON REAGAN

- 1981—The fifty-two American hostages are released on the day of President Reagan's Inauguration.

- 1981—Assassination attempt made on President Reagan, who makes a complete recovery.

- 1983—U.S. Embassy in Beirut is bombed.

- 1984—Reagan is reelected to a second full term in office.

- 1986—*Challenger* explodes on take-off.

- 1986—The IRS Code is overhauled.

- 1987—Reagan signs INF (Intermediate Range Nuclear Forces) Treaty with Premier Mikhail Gorbachev of the Soviet Union.

- 1987—In Germany, President Reagan demands of the Soviet Union: "Tear down this wall!"

GEORGE HERBERT WALKER BUSH (1924–)

State Born: Massachusetts   Occupation: Oil Businessman

Party: Republican   Religion: Episcopalian

GEORGE HERBERT WALKER BUSH

FORTY-FIRST PRESIDENT

1989–1993

To this day, like every parent who has lost a child, we wonder why; yet we know that, whatever the reason, she is in God's loving arms.

—GEORGE H.W. BUSH,
*on the death of his three-year-old
daughter, 1953*

T here are no atheists in foxholes or airplane cockpits." So goes an old military cliché. Anyone who has ever been in either of these situations can attest to the accuracy of the statement. President George H. W. Bush was no exception.

As a navy pilot during World War II, the young lieutenant was shot down in the Pacific. Ever since that memorable day, he has spoken boldly about his faith in Almighty God.

This was not to imply that the life-threatening incident was a conversion experience for President Bush. Religious teaching had always been a part of his home life. Either his mother, Dorothy Walker Bush, or father, Prescott Sheldon Bush, read a Bible lesson to

220

young George and the rest of the family each morning at the breakfast table. "We regularly attended at Christ Church (Episcopalian) in Greenwich, Connecticut," he wrote in his autobiography, *Looking Forward*.

George and Barbara Bush's religious convictions were never more tested than in 1953 when their three-year-old daughter, Robin, was diagnosed as suffering from leukemia. She died six months later. "Prayer had always been an important part of our lives," recalls the president, "but never more so than during those six months. Barbara and I sustained each other; but in the end, it was our faith that truly sustained us, as gradually, but surely, Robin slipped away. To this day, like every parent who has ever lost a child, we wonder why; yet we know that, whatever the reason, she is in God's loving arms."

A few months later, Bush told the junior high Sunday school class he taught that young Robin's death was just one example of the mysterious will of God.

The sovereignty of God—the view that nothing happens without his knowledge—dominated the personal theology of George H. W. Bush. Consequently, his presidency was one in which he insisted that his staff reflect the highest in moral standards.

Unlike his predecessor, President Bush was not shy about attending public worship. The former vestryman of St. Anne's Episcopal Church in Kennebunkport, Maine, kept a strong relationship with a variety of congregations—particularly with St. Martin's Episcopal in Houston, Texas, and Washington's National Cathedral where he held his membership during his tenure in the Oval Office. In fact, President Bush still counts as one of the highlights of his presidency the occasion on September 29, 1990, when he presided at the final stone-laying ceremony of the cathedral.

On the surface, President Bush appeared to be a spokesman for the more fundamentalist element of the Christian church. His conservative stances on abortion, women's rights, and civil rights seemed to be right out of the pages of a textbook written by televangelists Jerry Falwell or Pat Robertson. During the presidential campaign of 1988, he told a reporter that he was "born again." Yet he admitted he felt awkward using such terms and that he normally didn't speak the language of the so-called evangelicals.

DESERT STORM

Interpretation of language was not necessary on that memorable evening of January 16, 1991, when America launched into a war in the Persian Gulf commonly called Desert Storm. As a United Nations deadline for Iraq to withdraw from Kuwait was about to expire, President Bush telephoned Presiding Bishop Edmond Browning of the Episcopal Church and U.S. Senate Chaplain Richard Halverson. He told them that he had been praying for peace. Both prayed with him on the telephone.

On Wednesday morning, January 16, Bush called evangelist Billy Graham. "I need you," he said.

Graham, a longtime personal friend, arrived at the White House at about 5:45 p.m. Allied planes were already heading for Baghdad. Throughout the evening, the evangelist prayed five times, with Bush alone as well as with other members of the family.

The next day, at the White House, the president told congressional leaders: "There's a lot of prayer going on here, on Capitol Hill and across this whole country. And it will be that way until this [war] is concluded."

Desert Storm was over quickly—exactly one hundred hours after the ground war began. Yet, during this short time, quite possibly more prayers were offered by Americans than at any time in its history, and the loudest "Amens" came from the White House.

President George H. W. Bush, as did the thirty-nine men before him who placed their hands on a Bible and swore to "faithfully execute the office of the president of the United States," tried to uphold an individual sense of values without offending those whom he pledged to serve.

Following his retirement from public office, President Bush celebrated life by parachuting out of an airplane on his eightieth birthday and by seeing his son, George W. Bush, elected to the presidency in 2000 and reelected in 2004.

When the weight of responsibility takes its toll, when the tension mounts to a height greater than anyone should have to bear, when one crisis after another looms at the door of the Oval Office, for George Herbert Walker Bush, the oath with which he began his presidency will become more pronounced as his daily prayer: "So help me God."

HIGHLIGHTS OF THE ADMINISTRATION OF GEORGE HERBERT WALKER BUSH

- 1989—Bush sends U.S. troops to Panama against Manuel Noriega.

- 1989—The Berlin Wall falls.

- 1991—Desert Storm begins and ends.

- 1992—President Bush is defeated in his bid for reelection by Governor William Clinton.

WILLIAM JEFFERSON CLINTON (1946–)

State Born: Arkansas   Occupation: Lawyer

Party: Democrat   Religion: Baptist

WILLIAM JEFFERSON CLINTON

FORTY-SECOND PRESIDENT

1993–2001

On Sunday mornings, Bill Clinton attends church and is the incarnation of the president. On Saturday night, however, he's good ol' Bill.

—Dick Morris,
former advisor to President Clinton

Our forty-second president was a Rhodes Scholar from Georgetown University who studied at Oxford, later attended Yale University School of Law, and became a law professor. When he was only thirty-two he was elected as governor of Arkansas—for a total of five terms.

Bill Clinton's birth on August 19, 1946, in Hope, Arkansas, made him the first president born after World War II. He was named William Jefferson Blythe IV for his father, who had died three months prior to his birth in a traffic accident. When he was four, his mother, Virginia Cassidy, wed Roger Clinton of Hot Springs, Arkansas, and at the age of fifteen, Bill legally changed his last name to Clinton.

Young Bill spent a lot of time with his grandfather, who taught him that all people should be respected. From then on, Bill expressed regret and outrage at racism.

EARLY ASSOCIATION WITH THE CHURCH

Bill Clinton exhibited unusually solemn attitudes, however, toward his religion during his early years. Of his mother, stepfather, and stepbrother, Bill was the only one who attended church. He was baptized at Park Place Baptist Church in Hot Springs, and his mother recounted that he never missed a Sunday. Often she had to work, so on his own, he would pick up his Bible and walk to the church. The minister remembered thirteen-year-old Bill Clinton often waiting at the church before the minister arrived to open the doors.

During his terms as governor and president, Clinton remained a member of Little Rock Immanuel Baptist Church, which is affiliated with the Southern Baptist Convention.

ADVOCATE OF RELIGIOUS FREEDOM

President Clinton was not a fan of what has been called fundamentalist or evangelical Christianity. Even before personal scandals made headline news, he never went out of his way to court those more religiously conservative. However, he did advocate freedom for anyone to express his or her religious convictions. "The free exercise of religion has been called the first freedom, that which originally sparked the development of the full range of the Bill of Rights," Clinton said at the signing of the Religious Freedom Restoration Act of 1993. "Our founders cared a lot about religion. And one of the reasons they worked so hard to get the first amendment into the Bill of Rights . . . is that they well understood what could happen to this country, how both religion and government could be perverted if there were not some space created and some protection provided . . . freedom between government and people of faith that otherwise government might usurp."

In a 1994 radio interview on KMOX in St. Louis, the president said "You have never found me criticizing evangelical Christians. I have welcomed the involvement in our political system of all people and especially people of faith. I have bent over backwards as a governor and as a president to respect the religious convictions of all Americans. I have strong religious convictions myself."

PRAYER IN PUBLIC SCHOOLS

President Clinton strongly endorsed an opportunity for students in public schools to be able to pray and even study the Bible. He said in a radio address in December 1999, "Students do have the right to pray privately and individually in school, the right to say grace at lunch, the right to meet in religious groups on school grounds and to use school facilities just like any other groups do. They have the right to read the Bible or other religious books during study hall or free class time and the right to be free from coercion to participate in religious activity of any kind."

In a memorandum of July 1995, he addressed the same issue in even stronger terms:

It appears that some school officials, teachers and parents have assumed that religious expression of any type is either inappropriate, or forbidden altogether, in public schools.

However, nothing in the First Amendment converts our public schools into religion-free zones, or requires all religious expression to be left behind at the schoolhouse door. While the government may not use schools to coerce the consciences of our students, or to convey official endorsement of religion, the government's schools also may not discriminate against private religious expression during the school day.

SOME UNEXPECTED RELIGIOUS FUROR

On March 29, 1998, President and Mrs. Clinton visited a Roman Catholic Church in South Africa. The priest, Reverend Mohlomi Makobane, gave Holy Communion to the president of the United States, a Southern Baptist who worships at his wife's Methodist Church in Washington, D.C.

The policy of the Roman Catholic Church is that, except in extreme circumstances, only Catholics are to consume the consecrated bread and wine at a Mass. Father Makobane, therefore, was criticized for his action, as were President and Mrs. Clinton. The White House later sent a letter of apology, which stated that the Clintons had been invited to participate, and they regret any ill feelings that may have resulted from their visit.

NO FAVORITISM OF GOD'S BLESSINGS

Unlike many people who feel that God has a special plan for America, President Clinton revealed his personal insight at a White House interfaith breakfast in 1993:

It is very important that, as Americans, we approach this whole area with a certain amount of humility, that we be careful when we say that because we seek to know and do God's will, God is on our side and therefore against our opponent. That is important for two reasons. One is, we might be wrong. After all, we're only human. The other is that the thing that has kept us together over time is that our Constitution and Bill of Rights gives us all the elbow room to seek to do God's will in our own life and that of our families and our communities, and that means that there will be inevitable conflicts; so that there will never be a time when everything that we think is wrong can also be illegal. There will always be some space there because there will have to be some room for Americans of good faith to disagree.

OKLAHOMA CITY, 1995

On the morning of April 19, 1995, just after parents dropped their children off at day care at the Murrah Federal Building in downtown Oklahoma City, the unthinkable happened. A massive bomb inside a rental truck exploded, obliterating half of the nine-story building and killing 168 people in the worst terrorist attack on U.S. soil to that time.

Four days later, President Clinton stood before thousands of Oklahoma citizens with Governor Frank Keating and evangelist Billy Graham. All the remarks were meaningful, but the president gave the most pastoral comfort, as he seemed to reach back to the Sunday school lessons he learned as a youngster in Arkansas. "Let us teach our children that the God of comfort is also the God of righteousness. . . . Let us let our own children know that we will stand against the forces of fear. . . . As St. Paul admonished us, let us not be overcome by evil, but overcome evil with good."

BOTH SAINT AND SINNER

President Clinton, on one hand, could mesmerize crowds and persuade listeners to endorse his goals and visions with his folksy, but pointed, rhetoric. He paved the way for social changes, for a reform in Social Security, and enjoyed a bustling economy. He brought a vitality to the Oval Office that was reminiscent of his idol, John F. Kennedy.

On the other hand, Clinton's administration was marked by personal scandal accusations that he gave false testimony to a grand jury. This last charge led to his becoming the second president ever to be impeached. Although the U.S. Senate vote fell short of the two-thirds necessary for expulsion, this blemish on his record will remain a part of his legacy.

Perhaps this is one of the reasons that Clinton identified with so many people. He was no better than the rest of us. As Martin Luther once said, "Every one of us is both sinner and saint at the same time."

HIGHLIGHTS OF THE ADMINISTRATION OF WILLIAM JEFFERSON CLINTON:

- 1993—First attack is made on the World Trade Center.

- 1993—Clinton cuts taxes for low-income families.

- 1993—Clinton signs the Brady Bill.

- 1993—NAFTA is signed into law.

- 1993—Clinton starts AmeriCorps.

- 1994—Congress ratified the General Agreement on Tarrifs and Trade (GATT), committing the U.S. to the World Trade Organization

- 1995—Murrah Federal Building in Oklahoma City is bombed.

- 1996—Clinton wins second full term in office.

- 1996—Two U.S. Embassies in Africa are bombed.

- 1998—President Clinton becomes the second president to be impeached.

GEORGE WALKER BUSH (1946–)

State Born: Texas   Occupation: Businessman

Party: Republican   Religion: Methodist

GEORGE
WALKER BUSH

FORTY-THIRD PRESIDENT

2001–2008

*I feel like God wants me to run for president. I can't explain it, but I sense my
country is going to need me. Something is going to happen. I know it won't be
easy on my family, but God wants me to do it.*

—GEORGE W. BUSH

Not since Abraham Lincoln has a sitting president talked so much
about God as has George W. Bush. No president since Woodrow
Wilson has adopted the mantle of someone who has been elected by
Almighty God to do his will here on earth, as has George W. Bush.

To President Bush, "In God We Trust" is more than an imprint
on American currency; it is a conviction in his heart. He gave the
nation its first hint of the depth of this commitment during a
Republican presidential primary debate in 2000. When moderator
Bob Abernathy asked what person had the greatest influence on his
thinking, candidate Bush answered simply, "Christ, because he
changed my heart."

According to Howard Fineman in a *Newsweek* article appearing March 10, 2003, the Bush presidency is the most resolutely "faith-based" in modern times.

In April 2000, even as Texas governor, he raised more than one eyebrow when he proclaimed June 10, 2000, as Jesus Day urging Texans to "follow Christ's example by performing good works in their communities and neighborhoods." And the reason is that George W. Bush was, and still is, on a mission.

PLANTING OF A SEED

As a youth, George W. Bush held faith and religion at arm's length. Occasionally he attended the Episcopal church with his parents, and his marriage on November 5, 1977, to Laura Welch, was in a Methodist church. But the seeds of his decision to alter his lifestyle and attitude were planted by evangelist Billy Graham during a summer weekend visit with the Bush family in Maine. His father invited Graham to answer questions from the large contingent of family members, and while young Bush could not remember Graham's exact words, he later recalled, "The Lord was so clearly reflected in his gentle and loving demeanor." Bush believed that the Reverend Graham planted a seed in his soul, and he said, "This was the moment I would commit my heart to Jesus Christ."

A GROWING SPIRITUAL LIFE

One of the more noticeable changes in the life of George W. Bush was his decision to abstain from drinking alcohol. During his years in school, the young Bush seldom passed an opportunity to hoist a few quaffs of ale. In 1976, he was even cited for DUI. He soon realized that alcohol was not a positive dimension of his life. Quite to the contrary, in his opinion. Therefore, almost overnight, he quit drinking. Abstinence is a practice he maintains to this day.

As changes slowly emerged in his life, both George and Laura Bush became active members of the First Methodist Church of Midland, Texas. They participated in several family programs, including Dr. James Dobson's *Focus on the Family*.

Another spiritual influence on George W. Bush was Evangelist Arthur Blessit, whom Bush had heard preaching over the radio and was impressed enough to arrange for a meeting. Their frank discussion led George Bush, more than ever, to give himself totally and completely to Christ.

In the spring of 1984, Bush's longtime Midland friend and then secretary of commerce, Don Evans, invited Bush to join him at a men's community Bible study. Nearly 120 men regularly attended. "I looked forward to being with them," remembers Bush. "My interest in the Bible grew stronger and stronger, and the words became clearer and more meaningful."

This closeness with the Scriptures and the church led him to seek the Republican nomination as president of the United States. "I feel like God wants me to run for president," he told Christian television host James Robison. "I can't explain it, but I sense my country is going to need me. Something is going to happen. I know it won't be easy on my family, but God wants me to do it."

Bush went on to explain that he heard Pastor Mark Craig deliver a sermon on Moses and how God had called him to leadership. Moses ultimately did His bidding, leading his people, relying on God for strength and direction and inspiration.

"People are starved for leadership," Pastor Craig said, "starved for leaders who have ethical and moral courage."

Bush felt that God was calling him to a greater level of leadership:

There was no magic moment of decision. After talking with my family during the Christmas holidays, then hearing this rousing sermon, to make the most of every moment, during my inaugural church service, I gradually felt more comfortable with the prospect of a presidential campaign. My family would love me, my faith would sustain me, no matter what.

George W. Bush won a disputed election for president of the United States in 2000.

A Theocratic White House

From his first day in the Oval Office, President Bush read the Bible regularly, either from the *One-Year Bible* given to him by Don Evans, or different chapters he chose to study.

Along with regular reading of Scripture, President Bush admitted that he prayed every day. "I learned the power of prayer. I pray for guidance. I do not pray for earthly things, but for heavenly things, for wisdom and patience and understanding."

September 11, 2001

One of the favorite stories of President Bush in terms of the importance of his faith and that of the nation was about the man who owned a house. He saw a crack running up the wall of that house, so he hired the best painter he could find. The painter covered the crack with a thick coat of paint. Everything looked fine for a while, until the crack reappeared. The man hired another, more expensive, painter to paint over the crack. Again, the crack came back.

President Bush reminded his audiences that the man would never fix the crack until he first fixed the foundation.

His foundation truly was tested on September 11, 2001, when that morning two hijacked commercial airliners crashed into the World Trade Center in New York City. Within an hour, another plane flew into the Pentagon, and yet a fourth plane was diverted through a counterattack on the part of some brave passengers, sending it into the ground near Pittsburgh.

At a memorial service on September 14 in the Washington National Cathedral, the president gave assurance to America, and to the world, by quoting Romans 8:38: "Neither death nor life, nor angels nor principalities nor powers, nor things present nor things to come, nor height nor depth. . . shall be able to separate us from the love of God." Then he added, "May he bless the souls of the departed. May he comfort our own. And may he always guide our country."

God's Special Mission for America

Similar to President Ronald Reagan's insistence that America should always be a light unto the world, a city set on a hill, President Bush felt that Almighty God had a special calling for America. In 2003, he told a group of religious broadcasters in Nashville, Tennessee, that he could not serve as a governor or as president "if I did not believe in a divine plan that supersedes all human plans."

The president in a State of the Union address said, "Let us not pray for tasks equal to our strength. Let us pray for strength equal to our tasks. And that is our prayer today, for the strength in every task we face." His belief in that prayer was evident when, in August 2004, Bob Woodward on *60 Minutes,* asked the president, "Before declaring war on Iraq, did you consult with your father?" President Bush responded, "No. I consulted with a higher Father."

Controversy about the President's Faith

As with chief executives before him, not everyone in America endorsed the president's stands on issues. For some, he was far too conservative; for others, not conservative enough.

But George W. Bush never shied away from controversy either as governor or as president. If anything, a challenge to his faith appeared to galvanize his gumption. "My faith frees me to put the problem of the moment in proper perspective," he said. "It frees me to make decisions that others might not like. Frees me to try to do the right thing, even though it may not poll well."

THE PRESIDENT'S RELATIONSHIP WITH ISRAEL

Some of his political foes objected to the president's close association with Israel. They felt that America's strong tie with Israel invited others, especially those in the Middle East, to perceive that the United States was declaring war on them. But President Bush's association with the Holy Land was much more personal.

When both he and Laura Bush were in Israel in 1998, they visited the Holy City of Jerusalem, the Western Wall, and the Church of the Holy Sepulcher. They went to the Sea of Galilee and stood atop the hill where Jesus delivered the Sermon on the Mount. "It was an overwhelming feeling," he said, "to stand in the spot where the most famous speech in the history of the world was delivered. It was the spot where Jesus outlined the character and conduct of a believer and gave his disciples and the world the beatitudes, the golden rule, and the Lord's Prayer."

The people in Bush's party included four governors, one Methodist, two Catholics, a Mormon, and several Jewish-American friends. One of them suggested that someone read from the Scriptures. Bush, instead, chose to read the words to "Amazing Grace"—his favorite hymn.

HOPE FOR GOD TO SPEAK THROUGH HIM

On July 9, 2004, President George W. Bush revealed another goal as he spoke with a group of Old Order Amish in Lancaster County,

Pennsylvania, and made this provocative admission: "I trust God speaks through me. Without that, I couldn't do my job." When he prays the petition in the Lord's Prayer, "Thy will be done," he says he mentally adds, "through me."

Living in a threatening, post 9/11 world, many Christians derive comfort from the idea that the United States is under the leadership of a prayerful, Christian president. Today, it is not uncommon for a citizen to approach President Bush following one of his public appearances and say, "Mr. President, I pray for you and your family."

President Bush looks that person in the eye and responds, "That's the greatest gift you can give."

HIGHLIGHTS OF THE ADMINISTRATION OF GEORGE WALKER BUSH

- 2001—The World Trade Center and Pentagon are struck by airplanes piloted by terrorists.

- 2003—President Bush declares war on Iraq. The U.S., Great Britain, Australia, and Poland, along with thirty-one other countries invade Iraq.

- 2004—President Bush is reelected to a second full term in office.

EPILOGUE

There is an expression learned in high-school Latin class: *Vox populi vox Dei*—"The voice of the people is the voice of God." It's one of those adages that's quoted so often, we tend to accept it as gospel truth. But is it?

Is the conviction of the masses guaranteed to be divinely inspired simply because they unite to declare something to be true? If history has taught us anything it is that, sometimes, the masses are wrong. The masses cheered when Joan of Arc was executed. The masses saluted Adolf Hitler during his quest for world dominance. The masses even turned their backs on Jesus when he was hung on a cross.

A genuine leader is not one who finds out what's popular, then jumps to the front of the crowd and yells, "Follow me." Instead, a leader is one who understands what is right and, in spite of opposition, bravely attempts to turn the crowd in the right direction. Our most notable presidents often have had to do just that.

The question remains: "How are these presidents certain they know what is right?" The answer for most of our chief executives has been to turn to the God of our fathers. Through what they learn through the Bible and the strength gained through their prayers, they have led America to become the greatest nation in the world.

What does all this have to say about the rest of us? Let's draw upon history.

Thousands of years ago, the Lord named the Jews as His "chosen people." This selection did not make the Jews a perfect nation. It did, however, give to the inhabitants of Israel a much greater responsibility.

The same holds true with America.

It may well be that God has selected America to be his modern shining "city set on a hill." If so, each of its citizens bears a greater responsibility to present an image to other nations of the world that we have something much better than any other form of government. We are not perfect. However, we strive to do what is right. To drape the American flag over the cross of Calvary, however, is a mistake. This would imply that every action taken by the United States is an extension of the will of God. In fact, it was this sort of crusade mentality that led the zealots of the Spanish Inquisition to commit unspeakable acts of cruelty.

America has been and remains a great nation chiefly because we the people have never been afraid to proclaim, "In God we trust!" It is not that we seek to have God on our side. Instead, we pray that we shall always be on the side of God.

To this end, may God bless America!

PRESIDENTIAL
CHURCH
AFFILIATIONS

(Listed by denomination whenever appropriate)

BAPTIST (4)

J. Carter	W. Harding
W. Clinton	H. Truman

CONGREGATIONALIST (1)

C. Coolidge

DISCIPLES OF CHRIST (3)

J. Garfield
L. Johnson
R. Reagan

EPISCOPALIAN (8)

G. H. W. Bush	F. Pierce
G. Ford	F. Roosevelt
J. Madison	J. Taylor
J. Monroe	G. Washington (by attendance)

METHODIST (3)

G. W. Bush
W. McKinley
J. Polk

PRESBYTERIAN (6)

J. Buchanan	B. Harrison
G. Cleveland	A. Jackson
D. Eisenhower	W. Wilson

QUAKER (2)

H. Hoover	R. Nixon

REFORMED (2)

T. Roosevelt	M. Van Buren

ROMAN CATHOLIC (1)

J. Kennedy

UNITARIAN (4)

J. Adams	M. Fillmore
J. Q. Adams	W. Taft

UNAFFILIATED (8)

C. Arthur	T. Jefferson
U. Grant	A. Johnson
W. Harrison	A. Lincoln
R. Hayes	Z. Taylor

ABOUT THE AUTHOR

John McCollister graduated with a B.A. in history from Capital University in Columbus, Ohio, and earned his Master of Divinity from Trinity Lutheran Seminary. While serving congregations in Michigan, he earned his Ph.D. in Communications from Michigan State University.

In 1982, McCollister was invited to give the Lincoln Day Address in Washington, D.C.

Dr. McCollister has served as a university professor and administrator and currently lives at the Spruce Creek Fly-In near Daytona Beach. He is the author of twenty-one books on the subjects of religion, history, aviation, and baseball.

NOTES ON RESEARCH

The author spent years researching the material for this book. As a graduate of Capital University with a major in American History and after completing requirements for his Ph.D. in Communications at Michigan State University (with a concentration on the speaking styles of American presidents), he is familiar with the expressions of faith uttered by those who have occupied the Oval Office.

In addition, the author has visited presidential libraries throughout this nation in search of records that reveal insights into the religious affiliations of the presidents. He has also interviewed those who were willing to share their observations about the presidents they knew. Those with whom he spoke include Mr. Clement Conger, former curator of the White House; Dr. Richard Halverson, chaplain of the U.S. Senate; Senator Paula Hawkins; Dr. Edward L.R. Elson, former chaplain of the Senate; and various clergymen of the churches attended by the presidents.